SECRETS OF
SHOTOKAN KARATE

by

Robin L. Rielly

Tuttle Publishing
Boston • Rutland, VT • Tokyo

First published in 2000 by Tuttle Publishing, an imprint of Periplus Editions (HK) Ltd, with
editorial offices at 153 Milk Street, Boston, Massachusetts 02109.

Library of Congress Cataloging-in-Publication Data

Rielly, Robin L.
    Secrets of shotokan karate / Robin L. Rielly.
        p. cm.
    ISBN 0-8048-3229-3
    1. Karate I. Title.
    GV1114.3.R56 2000
    796.815'3--dc21   99-41593
                                                            CIP

Distributed by

USA   JAPAN
Tuttle Publishing   Tuttle Publishing
Distribution Center   RK Building, 2nd Floor
Airport Industrial Park   2-13-10 Shimo-Meguro, Meguro-Ku
364 Innovation Drive   Tokyo 153 0064
North Clarendon, VT 05759-9436   Tel: (03) 5437-0171
Tel: (802) 773-8930   Fax: (03) 5437-0755
Tel: (800) 526-2778

CANADA   SOUTHEAST ASIA
Raincoast Books   Berkeley Books Pte Ltd
8680 Cambie Street   5 Little Road #08-01
Vancouver, British Columbia   Singapore 536983
V6P 6M9   Tel: (65) 280-1330
Tel: (604) 323-7100   Fax: (65) 280-6290
Fax: (604) 323-2600

First edition
06 05 04 03 02 01 00   10 9 8 7 6 5 4 3 2

Design by Peter Holm, Sterling Hill Productions
Printed in the United States of America

Dedicated to my teacher
MASTER TERUYUKI OKAZAKI

Contents

Illustrations

Preface

In the past two decades numerous karate training manuals have appeared in English, all attempting to achieve the same goal. That is, they strive to transmit to Western martial artists the principles so readily understood by their Eastern teachers. This is a difficult task. In past years, many of the Japanese instructors who came here found the language barrier a formidable obstacle as they attempted to spread their art to their American students. In many cases, students were lost as a result of this inability to communicate the essence of difficult physical and psychological principles.

Since the first Japanese instructors migrated to the United States to spread their art, enough time has passed to overcome this problem. In their four decades of instruction here, they have produced students who have an understanding of the art that they are attempting to spread. This is fortunate for present-day students of karate, who will find it much easier to learn the techniques and the principles behind them.

The genesis of this book springs from a desire on my part to assist my instructor in spreading the art of karate in the Western world. It has been my good fortune to have trained regularly with many top Japanese instructors over the last four decades. The most notable of them has been Master Teruyuki Okazaki, Chairman of the International Shotokan Karate Federation. It is primarily because of his teaching and influence that this work has been produced.

There is an additional concern relative to martial arts in America. As we survey the development of karate in this country, it becomes obvious that it has gone off track. Many individuals claim to hold extremely high rank in relatively new organizations. A cursory examination of their credentials, background, and training indicates that many are marginally qualified to teach the arts in which they claim mastery. Countless thousands of students pay tuition at their schools and adhere to their teachings, and in the end these students suffer from their instructors' lack of knowledge. The traditional karate schools, by comparison, produce students with a solid knowledge of the techniques and principles described in this manual. Since these organizations are basically closed systems, the knowledge that their students have remains with them. It is my hope that this situation will open up so that all Americans practicing karate will be able to improve their techniques, regardless of style, system, or organization. Only in that way can America's karate develop to its maximum.

Virtually all authors owe debts of gratitude for assistance in completing their work. I wish to thank my students and assistant instructors at the Kobukan Karate Club in Toms River, New Jersey, for their help in posing for the many photographs that illustrate this manual. Among them are: John Kandes, Tom Finnerty, Glenn Rosenthal, Joe Schoenig, Robert Todaro, and Ed Winters. Glenn Rosenthal and Clifford Day kindly consented to proofread the manuscript, and my wife, Lucille, assisted with the photography.

I am also indebted to the Philadelphia Museum of Art for the work of art from their collection, appearing on page 4.

In addition, Master Masatoshi Nakayama, Chief Instructor of the Japan Karate Association, kindly consented to allow the use of his calligraphy on pages 6 and 90.

CHAPTER ONE

Basic Physical-Psychological Principles

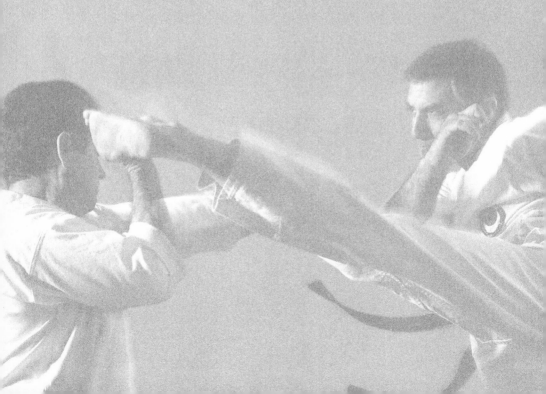

Zen and the Martial Arts

The long and secretive history of the Asian martial arts is replete with references to Zen Buddhism and Zen principles. The origins of these Zen influences can be traced back many centuries to the legendary travels of Bodhidharma, although many of the stories about him are questioned by historians.

According to the legends, Bodhidharma (Daruma Taishi in Japanese) was an Indian monk who was born into the warrior caste (*Kshatriya*). In his youth he was trained in the warrior's arts that were prevalent at the time. This included a weaponless form of fighting known as *vajramushti*. Eventually he began the study of Zen Buddhism under the Indian master Prajnatara. Later in his life he traveled to China to spread the Zen school of Buddhism. The date for this journey is also in dispute; however, most authorities assert that it took place around 520 A.D.

Once in China, Bodhidharma traveled throughout the country, eventually settling at the Shaolin monastery in Sung Shan. The rigors of the Zen Buddhism that he taught proved excessive for the monks, and in order to strengthen them physically, he included martial arts training, similar to that which he had undergone in India. This training became the basis for the fighting systems developed at the monastery, systems that also enabled the monks to defend themselves against bandits. Since that time, karate and Zen have been inexorably intertwined, and no traditional karate school is without a Zen influence.

Chinese-style karate eventually spread to Okinawa and Korea, where the Zen influence was transferred along with

Plate 1 Two studies of a Buddhist monk by Hokusai. Photo courtesy of the Philadelphia Museum of Art: Purchased through the Taylor Fund.

the physical art. Eventually, in the twentieth century, karate was spread to Japan proper by Okinawan masters such as Gichin Funakoshi, Chojun Miyagi, and Kenwa Mabuni. Once established there, it was influenced by the native fighting systems, notably *jujitsu* and *kenjitsu*.

These Japanese combative systems already had a strong Zen influence, dating to the beginnings of Zen Buddhism in Japan in the twelfth century. This introduction of Zen into Japan took place roughly about the same time that the warrior caste (*samurai*) came into power.

Within a century, the value system of the Zen Buddhists had influenced the samurai. Ultimately those who became top sword and spear masters were buoyed in their training by the ability to concentrate during combat, achieving a state of mind known as *mushin* (no-mind). This mental condition enabled the warrior to block out all thought of death and concentrate completely on his technique.

As time wore on and Japan became a unified nation under the Tokugawa clan (c. 1600), the need for combat-ready warriors lessened. The training in technique and Zen intensified, and warriors no longer called upon to fight in clan wars attempted to refine and perfect their fighting techniques. This led to advances in martial arts techniques and ultimately to a greater emphasis on Zen training in the martial arts.

By the time karate was introduced to Japan proper in the early twentieth century, the Zen tradition in martial arts was so strong that practically every martial artist strove to perfect his technique by using Zen concentration. When Zen-influenced karate was introduced from Okinawa, it was readily accepted into the family of Japanese martial arts. Virtually all classical karate systems today keep the Zen tradition, and its principles underlie all of them.

Zen and Karate

Much has been made of the relationship between karate and Zen Buddhism; however, it seems that many students who wish to master karate fail to comprehend the connection. They still seek verbal answers to that which must be understood nonverbally.

To begin with, an instructional manual of this sort is not really in keeping with the Zen tradition in martial arts. In martial arts training in the past, a student simply learned a technique from his teacher and then commenced to practice it vigorously. A request for an explanation as to how the technique might be used, or the reason for doing it a certain way, would usually be answered with a Zen-type of response:

"Train three years and then ask." If the student still had the temerity to ask at the end of the three years, the answer would be the same. In short, there is no satisfactory way of verbally explaining techniques that compares to understanding gained through self-discovery. An instructor can stand in front of a student and tell him repeatedly that his rising block is too low, and still the student never seems to correct it. But if the instructor swings a *kendo shinai* at the student's head and

the block is still too low, it will become immediately apparent to the student that there is a flaw in his blocking technique. Students who receive such a crack on the head quickly learn through experience how to properly execute a block. This method of training follows the principles of Zen in that one learns through experience, rather than through verbal instruction.

Plate 2 *Ken Zen Ichinyo* (The fist and zen are the same). Calligraphy by karate master Masatoshi Nakayama, presented to the Kobukan Karate Club.

Is this type of training to be preferred over the lengthy verbal explanations and references to training manuals? In the present

day, particularly in the West, traditional training would discourage many students, even those who think they will become Zen experts in the process of learning karate. Perhaps that is one reason why few true martial arts experts are produced in the Western world. Trends in present-day karate training seem to be away from Zen practices. Today, the average karate student, particularly outside Japan, receives detailed explanations about how techniques should be performed and why. This produces karate practitioners who have great knowledge of theory, but perhaps little feeling for the art they practice. It may be that Zen-type karate training is not suitable for Westerners. In determining if this is true, a consideration of the circumstances of present-day training is necessary.

Many small, nonprofit clubs exist—however, they need space to train, and that space must be rented. This produces a dilemma for instructors who must ensure that there will be enough students so that the karate club can afford to pay the rent. Since money becomes a consideration, it is necessary to keep students. Many would quit if exposed to old-style training methods which, although preserving the true tradition of Zen martial arts, place little value on retaining large numbers of students. This problem was recognized by Japanese instructors who attempted to teach Westerners in Japan after World War II and by the karate instructors who came here in the early 1960s.

Training in those years was somewhat different from that of the present day. American students who trained with Japanese instructors in the 1960s knew better than to ask for explanations. They would either receive a Zen-type reply or a crack over the head with the kendo shinai. This left them with the choice of quitting practice or continuing to train while seeking the answers for themselves. Many quit. By the end of the 1960s, it had become apparent that authentic Japanese karate was not expanding greatly, so some changes in training methods were made. More verbal explanations were given for techniques, and students were able to get answers to questions readily, without practicing for years. This change, of course, was not in keeping with tradition. The question then, is whether the new style of training is superior or inferior to the old. In all likelihood, the end results will be the same; the main difference is that more people will remain in karate training, and the number of Zen-type trainees will continue to grow. The answer to the question, then, is that today's training is not better or worse, just different. If the goal of karate training is to develop self-discipline and self-control in people, then it is necessary to keep students in training in order to accomplish the task. Making training harder and less understandable will not achieve that goal.

Stimulus and Response

All of fighting may be viewed as a process of stimulus and response. This is a relatively simple concept to understand, even for the layman. As it relates to karate, it involves the tendency of an individual to respond to actions not initiated by himself. In other words, when attacked, an individual responds by defending himself. The attack is the stimulus and the defense the response. Consequently, it follows that training should attempt to reinforce and develop, as much as possible, the ability of the individual to respond to outside stimuli. While sparring drills demand such a reaction, there are still other methods of training that will benefit the student in this regard.

Formal karate training usually takes place in a class atmosphere, with the instructor giving commands and instruction, and then counting as the students perform each exercise. Many fail to realize that this is the perfect time to train the stimulus-response process. The voice of the instructor may be viewed as the stimulus, and the student's individual movement in the course of training is the response to it.

Students begin each drill in the *zanshin*, or ready, position. At the command *kamae-te* from the instructor, they are supposed to shift forward into a downward blocking position.

Beginners frequently have to be told to recover their ready position and begin again, moving more quickly than the first time. Some think the instructor simply wants them to move faster, but what is desired is that they accelerate their response to the instructor's voice stimulus.

Basic training requires the student to march back and forth, punching, kicking, and blocking at the air, and it is necessary to train the stimulus-response process against a voice command, since there is no actual opponent. Students are told by the instructor to imagine an opponent in front of them at all times. By doing this, students benefit from training more than if they don't "see" an opponent at all. Such concentration on an imaginary opponent makes the practice of techniques much more realistic, and the students actually put more into and receive more from their training. The voice command of the instructor, coupled with the imaginary opponent visualized by the student, provides the necessary stimulus for valuable training to take place. Therefore, it is necessary for the student to listen closely for the instructor's count, and to immediately execute the next technique when he hears the count. This will aid in later sparring practice, since the stimulus-response ability has been developed in basic training.

In sparring drills, the use of stimulus and response is simple to practice. All the basic sparring drills are centered around the proper response to an attack, whether it be shifting, dodging, or blocking and countering the attack. Once this ability has been mastered through basic training and sparring drills, the responses of the fighter in free sparring will be automatic. Thus it is necessary to practice basic sparring drills continually, in order to develop automatic responses. Those who simply train in free-sparring and neglect the myriad of drills available to them will not be able to reach their full potential as fighters.

Stimulus and response training is also possible in *kata*, except that it is much more difficult. If an instructor is counting as the student performs each move in the kata, then the voice may be used as stimulus. However, in the free performance of kata, the practitioner must create the stimulus in his or her own mind by imagining an attack and responding to it. This stimulus and response reaction is extremely difficult to attain in the early stages of training. When such a stage is reached in kata practice, performers truly feel the presence of attackers and their concentration is so developed that they will find it easy to sense the attacks of actual opponents. This is one of the reasons why karate practitioners in the past spent so much time in the practice of a single kata. It enabled them to devote full concentration to each movement and develop the ability to provide their own stimulus to which they could respond.

Kime

Kime, or focus, is the prime ingredient in the generation of force in karate techniques. It is a combination of physical and psychological factors resulting in maximum power in karate blocks, kicks, punches, and strikes. Kime is achieved by instantaneously tensing the muscles of the entire body for a split second at the moment of impact. This tension should be coordinated with a sharp exhalation of air and total mental concentration on the area of impact at the moment contact is made with the opponent.

In general, kime lasts only a fraction of a second, since to hold tension in the body past the instant of contact with a target area would not add to the force generated. In addition, such tension would slow down the transition to the next move.

Kiai

The *kiai*, or spirited yell, is usually performed as a technique is executed. If done properly, the kiai will add force to the technique. Unlike most sounds human beings make, the kiai is not generated in the throat, but rather in the lower abdomen. It is usually performed by tensing the stomach muscles while sharply exhaling. The sound that is heard should be "eh," "yah," or "to." It is a monosyllabic grunt, rather than a word.

For combat purposes, the kiai serves three functions. First of all, a loud noise, properly made, will startle an opponent and possibly create an opening in his defenses. Second, it will give a psychological lift to the performer, helping to build his spirit. Last, the kiai requires that the breath be exhaled and the stomach muscles tensed, adding force to a technique or preparing the body to absorb a blow from an opponent.

Plate 3 The author assists Master Masatoshi Nakayama as he demonstrates the rising block. Master Teruyuki Okazaki looks on.

CHAPTER TWO

Principles of
Physical Movement

Figure 1   Figure 2   Figure 3

Figure 4   Figure 5   Figure 6

Figure 6a   Figure 7   Figure 8

Natural Body Movement

One of the major problems that many karate practitioners have is overcoming awkward movement as they perform karate techniques. In many cases awkward movement is the direct result of a failure to follow the natural movement of the body.

Our muscles are trained daily to operate in an efficient manner that makes it possible to walk and perform a number of physical tasks effectively and with a minimum expenditure of energy. Such movements usually are smooth and effortless, since the body is used to them. In the practice of karate techniques, in fact in all physical endeavors, adherence to these normal patterns of movement is necessary in order to perform at our best.

Let us consider the natural movement of the body as it walks forward (See Figures 1–4). As seen from the front, the normal position of the body is one in which it is balanced evenly on both feet and held erect, with the feet about the same width apart as the shoulders (Fig. 1). As seen from the side, the erect position is obvious (Fig. 2). As the model steps forward with his right foot, it is apparent that the movement begins with the hip rotating forward; the upper leg moves next, and finally the lower leg and foot (Figs. 3–4). This should be no mystery to the reader, and simply walking forward will verify that this is the manner in which movement is accomplished. It follows then, that in order for a karate movement to follow the natural movement of the body it

Figure 9   Figure 10   Figure 11

Figure 12   Figure 13   Figure 14

Figure 15   Figure 16   Figure 17

must follow the same sequence of movements: hip, upper leg, and finally lower leg.

Figures 5 through 6A demonstrate the body's forward movement. In the beginning position (Fig. 5), the upper body is naturally upright and the feet shoulders' width apart. As the model steps forward, the hips move first, followed by the upper and then the lower leg. Any other sequence of movement would be awkward. The principle to be understood here is that the hip must move first, and the upper body must be in its natural erect position.

When one is stepping in a new direction, the head turns in that direction as one looks to see where one is going (Figs. 7–8). The hips then rotate in that direction (Fig. 9), and the upper leg, lower leg, and foot follow (Fig. 10).

A natural body position is usually the beginning point for basic drills and katas. As demonstrated in Figure 11, the feet are about the same width apart as the shoulders, and the inside of the knee is directly above the inside edge of the foot. It follows then that in the basic stances this positioning should also be the case. In Figure 12 a stick is used to demonstrate the line between the inner knee and the inner edge of the foot. In the front stance (Fig. 13), the line should remain vertical.

As the body moves forward in the front stance, the feet begin and end shoulder width apart. In order to follow natural movement, the hips move first (Figs. 14–15). This is also the case with the front kick (Fig. 16). The hips move forward first, the upper leg and knee are raised, and the foot is snapped forward to perform the kick (Figs. 16–17).

Note that in performing multiple kicks hip movement must also be in the direction of the kick. Figures 18 and 19 show the front kick, with the hips facing forward. The performance of the side kick (Figs. 20–21) gains power when the hip is thrust

Figure 18 **Figure 19** **Figure 20**

Figure 21 **Figure 22** **Figure 23**

Figure 24 **Figure 25** **Figure 26**

in the direction of the kick. The back thrust-kick (Figs. 22–24) requires that the hip position be maintained in order to execute the kick properly.

When an opponent approaches from the side, it is necessary to face the hips in that direction in order to kick at him. In this case the roundhouse kick is used after the hips are turned in the direction of the opponent (Figs. 25–28).

Balance and Stability

Common sense would dictate that balance is an essential ingredient in any successful athletic movement, and particularly relevant in combat situations. An examination of some of the factors affecting balance is therefore necessary.

The body at rest adopts what we refer to as a natural position, that is a position in which the feet are spaced approximately shoulder width apart, with the weight of the body distributed evenly on them. It follows, then, that whenever possible, karate stances should follow this principle. Depicted in Figure 29 is the front stance. Note that the feet are placed approximately shoulder width apart for balance; failure to do so will affect the performer's balance. In Figure 30 the feet in

Figure 27   **Figure 28**   **Figure 29**

Figure 30   Figure 31   Figure 32

Figure 33   Figure 34

Figure 35   Figure 37

Figure 36   Figure 38

the front stance are in line and the body is difficult to balance, since the base of support is narrowed. It should also be noted that the upper body is held erect, and the hips in their normal position are in line with the rest of the body.

In Figure 31, the cat-foot stance is demonstrated. Balance here is difficult since the weight of the body is carried primarily on the rear leg. Still, it is possible to maintain balance, since the forward foot extends the base of support, and the knee is bent, lowering the hips. In addition, the upper body forms a straight line with the hip, affording maximum balance in this stance. Compare this with Figure 32. The model here deliberately has adopted a faulty cat-foot stance. Note that the upper body seems to lean backward slightly, upsetting the balance since hip and back are not in alignment. In addition, the knee is straightened, lessening the body's ability to balance correctly. If the performer were attacked in this position, he would likely lose balance to the rear if his opponent charged into him.

Figures 33 and 34 demonstrate how the misalignment of hip and back can cause a loss of balance. The balanced position in the straddle stance is one in which the upper body is straight, as compared to Figure 34, where the upper body inclines to the rear in an unbalanced position.

One of the subtleties of body movement affecting balance is the manner in which the feet are positioned against the floor. In Figures 35 through 38 correct and incorrect methods of using the feet are demonstrated. In order to maintain solid balance in any stance, it is necessary to tense the foot and toes downward as if trying to grip the floor with them, as demonstrated from the front and side in Figures 36 and 38. Figures 35 and 37 show an incorrect tension of the feet with the toes actually raised, causing less of the foot surface to contact the floor, and upsetting balance.

These may seem to be minor points as far as fighting technique is concerned; however, it must be remembered that balance affects all karate movement, and an unbalanced fighter is incapable of delivering the strongest technique.

Generating Force

The generation of force in karate techniques is a complex matter, combining a number of coordinated principles and movements, including hip movement, centrifugal force,

Figure 39   **Figure 40**

Figure 41   **Figure 42**

reaction force, leg drive, proper muscle use, speed, and focus. To accomplish this, the body must be maintained in the correct position for each technique so that the coordination of these principles and movements is maximized. Figure 39 demonstrates some of the factors adding to the generation of power in the counterpunch. The fighter stands in the left front stance, executing a counterpunch with the right fist. The punch commences with a sharp rotating motion of the hips (A). This rotation of the hips is aided by the driving force of the leg (B). As the punching fist travels forward (E), the opposite arm is withdrawn sharply (D), causing the shoulders to rotate in the same direction as the hips and adding reaction force to the punching arm (E). As the punch makes contact with the opponent, the rear leg is stiffened, adding a reaction force (C) to the punch.

Similar force is gained in the execution of some hand movements, using hip rotation opposite from that of the counterpunch. This type of reversed rotation may be observed in the rising block, inside block, downward block, knife-hand block, back-fist strike, and other hand techniques. Figure 40 demonstrates this reversed hip rotation in the performance of the rising block. The block begins with the rotation of the hip (A), to which is added the reaction force of the withdrawn hand (D). The driving force of the rear leg (B) creates a reaction force (C) that is added to the power of the blocking arm (E).

The power of the hip is also added to kicking techniques, as demonstrated in Figure 41. As the front kick is thrust forward, the hip is rotated in the direction of the kick (A). At the same time the supporting leg is thrust against the floor (B), creating a reaction force (C) that adds to the power of the kick.

In the roundhouse kick (Fig. 42), the power of the hips is

added to the kick by rotating the hip in the direction of the kick (A, D). The supporting foot must be turned in the same direction in order to facilitate the kick (B). In order for the kicker to keep balance, the upper half of the body must rotate in a direction opposite to the hip.

Coordinating Body Movement

In the execution of karate techniques it is necessary to coordinate all body movements, in order to produce maximum power. This means that the directional movement of the body must be coordinated with hand and foot movements to maximize the effect of a kick, punch, or block. In schools where the instructors are lacking in basic knowledge, ignorance of this principle seems to be common. Many of these unqualified instructors produce students whose body movements are grossly uncoordinated. Some of the most common errors can be observed when these students complete a step forward and then follow with a punch or block. In other cases, the student shifts into a stance, and after body movement has been completed, the arm movement follows. Any physical education instructor not versed in karate technique could spot these

Figure 43

Figure 44

coordination errors. A similar lack of coordination might be observed in a baseball player's batting technique. If the batter were to step toward the pitch and rotate his hips without moving the bat, and then, having completed the hip rotation, begin to swing the bat, the error would be obvious. No body power would be added to the swing, and the resultant hit would not have the full power of the batter.

Demonstrated next is the manner in which the hand, foot, and body movements must be coordinated in order to produce maximum power in the lunge punch. A similar process is necessary for blocks, strikes, and kicks. In Figure 43 the attacker (left) faces his opponent. Both are in sparring stances. The attacker steps forward in the front stance with his right foot, completing the step (Fig. 44). His right hand has begun the lunge punch, but has not completed it. The hand technique is not completed until after the step has been terminated (Fig. 45). This method of punching has divided the power generated by the body's forward movement from that developed by the hand in the completion of the punch. The result is a loss of power in the lunge punch.

In Figures 46 through 48 the attacker has completed the punch before his body motion has stopped. Beginning in the

Figure 45

left front stance (Fig. 46), he steps forward to begin a lunge punch, but his hand is fully extended in the punch before his body movement stops (Fig. 47). In the last photo (Fig. 48), the attacker has completed the step, but it has not been coordinated with the punch, and the

Figure 46   **Figure 47**

combined power of body movement and hand movement has not been achieved.

Figures 49 and 50 demonstrate the correct method of utilizing hand and body power. The attacker begins in the left front stance (Fig. 49) and then steps forward with his right foot to execute a right lunge punch (Fig. 50). Note that his foot has advanced, but his hand has not begun the punch. This is necessary, since hand movement is much quicker than body movement. In Figure 51 we see the completion of the punch. Maximum force has been developed, since the hand and foot have reached their terminal position at the same time.

This coordination of body movement is possible in both

Figure 48   **Figure 49**

Figure 50   **Figure 51**

forward and backward movements. The key to developing power in both directions is to make sure that the hand and foot stop at the same time.

Hip Movement and Centrifugal Force

A basic understanding of the physical forces that affect karate movements is necessary in order to achieve maximum power in techniques. Many karate practitioners fail to understand them and thus do not reach their full potential in regard to the amount of force that they generate. One such physical force is centrifugal force.

As demonstrated in previous sections, reaction force is generated in a kick, punch, or block by withdrawing the opposite arm or leg. This sharp movement usually causes some rotation movement in the hip. However, if a rotating movement is initiated by the hip as the punch is executed, then centrifugal force will be added to the reaction force, producing the strongest possible punch. An easy comparison is the swing of a batter as he attempts to hit the ball. Although coordination of the batter's swing has been discussed above, it should also be noted that a batter who does not rotate his hips and body

Figure 52   Figure 53   Figure 54

Figure 55   Figure 56   Figure 57

into the swing of the bat will have a very weak swing. Baseball fans can observe this easily, and recognize that the same principle applies to many other athletic movements, including karate punches, kicks, and blocks.

Shown in Figures 52 through 54 is the basic method of rotating the hip. Note that the hip position is forward in Figure 52 and then twisted to the side in Figure 53. This is the normal attitude of the body in executing a block, and is called the half-facing position. In Figure 54 the hip has been snapped forward as it would be in the execution of a punch. It is important to note that the position of the feet and knees does not change — only the hip moves.

To demonstrate that such force does exist, it is only necessary to try a simple experiment, as shown in Figures 55 through 57. Begin in the left front stance with the hip turned sideways. The arms must dangle loosely at the sides. Snap the hips forward (Figs. 56–57). The arms will be flung in a counterclockwise movement by the centrifugal force generated by the hip movement. Once this principle is understood, it is simply a matter of training to incorporate this force into karate techniques. If the hip rotation is performed slowly, the hands will not fly outward. Thus it may be observed that centrifugal force is directly affected by the speed of the hip's rotation

Reaction Force

One of the primary methods of generating power in a punch, kick, or block is the use of reaction force. This is simply a common-sense application of physics. That is to say that for every action there is an opposite and equal reaction. As applied to karate, this principle is easy to demonstrate.

Figure 58   Figure 59   Figure 60

Figure 61   Figure 62   Figure 63

Figure 64   Figure 65   Figure 66

Figures 58 through 61 show the basic counterpunch. The model stands in the left front stance, left hand out and right hand poised at the hip, ready to punch (Fig. 58). As the right hand begins its path toward the target, the left hand is withdrawn sharply to the side (Figs. 59–60). Failure to withdraw the hand sharply leads to a loss in power. Were the hand not withdrawn at all, the loss in punching power would be significant. The faster the hand is withdrawn, the harder the opposite reaction — the punch. Figure 61 demonstrates the reverse, with the right hand withdrawn and the left hand performing a jab, utilizing reaction force to propel the left hand forward. Figures 62 through 64 demonstrate the punch from a front view.

Similar force may be utilized in blocking. In Figures 65 through 68 the counterpunch has been completed and the model begins to withdraw the right hand as the left hand is moved upward in a rising block. Again, the speed with which the opposite hand is withdrawn determines how much reaction force is generated into the blocking arm.

This particular type of movement is commonly known as "draw hand" technique. It is one of the basic elements that examiners judge when students take the first-degree black belt

Figure 67   **Figure 68**

Figure 69

Figure 70

Figure 71

Figure 72

Figure 73

Figure 74

Figure 75

Figure 76

exam, although it should be developed prior to that time. Failure to demonstrate the use of such "draw hand" technique and the proper utilization of reaction force is sure to guarantee failure on the *shodan* exam.

It is also possible to use reaction force in kicking technique. As shown in Figures 69 through 75, the hip shift is used to generate reaction force into the front kick. The performer begins by shifting the left leg backward until it is almost in line with the right (Fig. 70). This rapid movement of the left leg generates reaction force into the kick of the right leg. It is essential to make sure that the motion of the leg being withdrawn causes a rapid movement of the hip (hip snap), generating reaction force in the kick. In Figures 72 through 75 the right leg is withdrawn and the left leg performs the kick. Training in such movements is a basic and invaluable method of developing power in karate techniques.

Leg Drive

One of the methods of adding force to a kick or punch is proper use of the driving leg. In this case the term "driving leg" refers to the forward thrust developed by correct use of the rear leg in a punching or kicking technique.

Figure 76 shows a basic counterpunch in the front stance. The arrow by the arm (A) indicates the direction of the punch, or for purposes of illustration, the direction of the force generated in the punch. As the punch travels forward to the intended target, additional force is generated by thrusting the rear leg against the floor. As shown by the arrow near the leg (B), the direction of the thrusting leg is upward, about 45 degrees. This leg force is added to the thrust generated by the upper body and hips in the execution of the punch. In general, this is why a

Figure 77

Figure 78

Figure 79

correctly executed punch in a long, low stance is more powerful than a punch delivered from a short, high stance.

The principle of leg drive works up to a certain point. If both forces could be aligned perfectly, this would not produce maximum power. In order to align both arm and leg, the performer would have to do a front split, a position that would be weak and ineffective. Alternately, the performer could punch upward at a 45-degree angle, thereby aligning the punching arm and leg (Fig. 77). Although this would increase power it would limit the performer's targets and might not be useful in all fighting situations. Research in this subject indicates that a leg angle of about 45 degrees provides maximum power. Once the leg is held at a lesser angle, force is lost because of decreased contact with the floor.

A low front stance of this type is useful for delivering a powerful blow; however, it is not as mobile as a shorter stance. A general principle to follow in fighting, therefore, is to fight in a higher stance, shift into a low stance to deliver a punch, and then immediately shift back to a higher stance to achieve greater mobility.

The same principle of leg drive applies in kicking techniques. The front thrust kick (Fig. 78), derives much of its power from the drive of the rear leg. If the angle of the supporting or drive leg is decreased from 90 degrees to nearer 45 degrees, the power of the kick will be increased. This assumes that the kick is aimed at the lower part of the body, so that the kicking leg will be nearly parallel with the floor upon termination of the technique. For kicks aimed at higher targets, the angle of the leg may be greater than 45 degrees and perhaps closer to 90 degrees, since the force is generated upward and forward (Fig. 79). In deciding how to use this principle to generate force in techniques, it must be remembered that theory

Figure 80

Figure 81

is not the sole determining factor in fighting. A lower angle of the leg in the kick, close to 45 degrees (Fig. 78) commits the kicker to a forward motion from which recovery is difficult, while a greater angle, closer to 90 degrees (Fig. 79) allows for greater mobility and the ability to escape a counterattack.

Theoretically then, greater force will be generated if the drive leg is closer to 45 degrees. This theoretical knowledge, however, must be balanced against other elements of fighting, such as mobility and shifting ability. In training for fighting it is necessary to understand the forces that generate power in a technique and to discover, through trial and error, how they may be utilized in actual combat.

Muscle Use

Correct use of the muscles in each technique is essential if maximum power is to be developed. Figure 80 shows the correct tensing of the muscles in the execution of punches. Note that the pectorals (A) are tensed, bringing the shoulder of the punching arm slightly forward. The latissimus dorsi muscles (B) are also tensed in order to keep the shoulder down. This enables the puncher to transfer the power of his or her body movement into the punching arm. At the same time the pectorals and latissimus dorsi muscles are tensed, the abdominals (C) are also tensed. This simultaneous tensing of the muscles of the front and side add power to the punch.

The correct tension of back muscles in the execution of blocks is seen in Figure 81. In this case, the back muscles must be contracted on both sides in order to add power to the blocking arm. Since the back muscles are tensed, it follows that the muscles in front of the body are slightly extended.

Muscle tension must be coordinated in order to perform rapid and powerful techniques. In the case of the straight punch, one set of muscles (primarily the triceps) must be tensed in order to straighten the arm and propel the fist forward. As the triceps are tensed, the biceps must be relaxed completely in order not to slow down the punch, since their work is opposed to that of the triceps. Tension in the biceps must be eliminated completely if maximum speed is to be achieved. The ability to tense specific muscles in a given technique is simply a matter of training. That is why athletes become faster and more efficient as the length of their training and experience increases.

Unnecessary muscle tension can also retard the ability to move rapidly into the next technique. In order to move efficiently, the muscles must be relaxed; only the specific ones used in the movement are tensed. Additionally, if muscle tension is held past the point of focus (kime), it can result in rapid muscle fatigue, and the fighter will tire before he should.

Focus

Focus (kime) is an essential element of power as it relates to fighting technique. Basically, focus is a combination of physical and psychological effort directed at the target area at the moment of impact. It is accomplished by exhaling sharply and tensing the stomach muscles, as well as the muscles of the entire body, instantaneously, as the target is contacted. Such split-second timing requires concentrated training in basics and, in particular, practice with the striking-post (*makiwara*). The muscle tension required to achieve focus lasts for only a split second, because there is no need to tense muscles before or after the completion of a given technique. Tension held longer than a split second merely wastes muscle energy and ultimately weakens technique.

Demonstrated below are some of the basic methods for practicing focus in various techniques. They all involve the use of the striking-post, although the use of this device is not necessary all the time. The striking-post serves a dual purpose in that, in addition to providing focus practice, it also allows the karate practitioner to actually hit something full force and get the feeling of making contact. As with all techniques, practice should be on both right and left sides.

Plate 4 Practicing the roundhouse kick against the makiwara.

The striking-post itself may be constructed in a number of ways, either by burying the post in the ground with adequate supports or by devising a stand to which it is fastened. Shown here is a post that has been fastened into a specially made stand and bolted to a 4 foot by 8 foot platform, allowing the entire unit to be moved. It is important that the striking post be constructed so that it has spring, allowing maximum force to be exerted in the technique. Some clubs fasten a pad directly to a wall, but this is unsuitable since it has no give.

Counter Punch

The model begins in the left front stance, with his right hand back and ready to punch (Fig. 82). His hips are turned to the side, and his body is in the side-facing position. He snaps his

Figure 82

Figure 83

Figure 84

Figure 85

Figure 86

Figure 87

hips forward and thrusts his right leg against the floor as he executes a counterpunch to the striking-post (Fig. 83). As his fist travels towards the target, he keeps the muscles of his body loose so that maximum speed may be attained. It is usually best to think of one's hip movement and forget about hand movement. This will allow the muscles of the arm and shoulder to relax and add speed to the technique. The practitioner exhales as the punching hand travels forward, tensing his or her entire body at the moment the fist impacts with the striking-post. The muscles are then immediately relaxed.

Knife-Hand Strike

Variation 1

The model begins in the straddle stance with his left foot closer to the striking-post. His left knife-hand is held alongside his right ear, palm inward (Fig. 84). He rotates his body slightly in a counterclockwise movement as he brings his left hand across the front of his body and strikes the post with the knife-edge of his left hand (Fig. 85). As he does this movement, he exhales sharply. As with all striking-post practice, the breath should be exhaled and the muscles tensed at the moment of impact. Note that as the knife-hand strikes the post, the palm is downward. It is also possible to practice the back fist strike from this position.

Variation 2

The model stands to the side of the striking-post in the left front stance. His right knife-hand is held high on the right side of his head (Fig. 86). He rotates his hips in a counterclockwise movement as he begins the movement. He strikes the post with the knife-edge of his hand (Fig. 87). Note that the palm is held upward.

Figure 88

Figure 89

Figure 90

Figure 91

Elbow Strike

The model begins in the front stance with his left foot forward. His right hand is held at his right hip (Fig. 88). He rotates his body in a counterclockwise movement as he performs the roundhouse elbow strike (Fig. 89). Other variations of the elbow strike may be practiced using the side stance.

Roundhouse Kick

In addition to practicing hand techniques against the striking-post, it is also possible to practice kicks. Although kicks are usually practiced against a bag, the roundhouse kick is a par-ticularly good one to practice against the striking-post.

The model stands in the left front stance at the side of the striking-post (Fig. 90). Using the ball of his foot, he kicks the post with a right roundhouse kick (Fig. 91).

Speed

One of the major factors in the generation of force is speed. This is obvious since the formula for force is mass 3 accelera-tion. For the karate practitioner, the development of speed is an essential part of training, not only in order to generate force, but to make it possible to avoid the opponent's attack and strike back before he can defend himself.

Although the limits of an individual's speed are to some extent determined by heredity, intensive training in karate movements will improve speed. This is a natural outgrowth of repetitive movement during training. In order to achieve max-imum speed in technique, it is essential that the body remain in as relaxed a state as possible, enhancing the ability of the body to move. Muscles that are prematurely tensed in the exe-cution of a technique serve only to slow down that technique,

Figure 92   **Figure 93**

Figure 94   **Figure 95**

and thus produce less force. The fighter who remains relaxed in his punching technique until the moment of impact will generate greater force than one who is stiff or tight.

Training for Power

Training in a technique differs somewhat from executing the same technique in the course of fighting. Such training is necessary in order to develop powerful movements.

Figures 92 through 95 demonstrate two ways in which the counterpunch is commonly executed. The first method (Figs. 92–93) has the fighter standing in a sparring stance and shifting forward to punch with his right hand. Note that the punching hand travels only a short distance to the target, as compared to the basic method of training in the counterpunch (Figs. 94–95). The logical question, then, is: Why is it necessary to practice long punching methods if they are not performed that way in actual combat?

The training method differs from the combat method because the longer motion of the punch is necessary to develop power. In combat only a short movement may be possible; however, if the punch is practiced only in that manner, it will not be possible to develop full power in the punch. Therefore, the method of training that utilizes a long movement will make it possible to execute a shorter movement with greater force.

Plate 5 The application of speed in karate technique is the direct result of arduous basic training.

Figure 96   **Figure 97**

Figure 98   **Figure 99**

This is also true in the training method for blocks. Figures 96 through 99 show the same principle as applied to the practice and execution of the downward block. If the training method for the block uses a long motion (Figs. 96–97), then the shorter combat-type of blocking motion (Figs. 98–99) will still have power.

CHAPTER THREE

Basic Elements of Fighting

Elements of Fighting

Traditional schools of karate spend a great deal of time practicing basic technique, basic sparring drills, and kata. The result is the production of students who have superb technique and a thorough understanding of karate and how it works. By contrast, some unqualified instructors spend little time on basics and kata and instead spend much of the students' practice time in free-sparring. This is a mistake. The ability to free-spar or fight well is the result of training, and should not be the primary means of training. In confusing cause and effect, such instructors virtually guarantee that their students will have limited progress in the martial arts. A skilled fighter must have proficiency in basic kicking, punching, blocking, striking, body shifting, distancing, speed, focus, timing, and perception of attack, coupled with experience and an understanding of the natural movement of his own body. When all of these elements are combined, the result is a karate practitioner who has the ability to spar effectively. All of these elements are to be found in numerous training methods described herein, and strict attention to their practice will aid the karate practitioner to become extremely proficient in sparring. In summation, sparring ability is the result of training, not the main type of training in which to engage. A discussion of how these elements fit together is required for understanding the process necessary to develop sparring proficiency.

Let us first consider basic kicking. Facing an opponent who suddenly presents an opening in his defense is a common occurrence for a fighter. All that is needed at that point, in order to become victorious, is the ability to place a kick or punch into the target area. This is easier said than done. If the opponent has superior speed or body shifting and blocking ability, the kicker may end up on the losing end of the

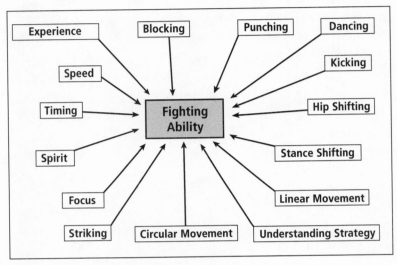

Plate 6 The components of fighting ability.

exchange. Only if the fighter's kicking speed and targeting ability are superior will he or she be able to score. How is this accomplished? The answer is quite simple, as it will be in the case of all the basic elements. The fighter must develop kicking ability through countless thousands of repetitions until the kick is fast and strong enough to score. Those who have neglected basic training in the kick — that is, numerous repetitions with proper form — will not have the ability to use a given kick or other technique against an opponent when an opening occurs. There is no easy way to accomplish this; it can only be done by repetition kicking. Such drilling in the basic kicks will enable the karate practitioner to have enough skill and confidence in his kick to be able to strike an opponent when the opportunity presents itself.

Basic punching and striking practice will provide the same ability and confidence with hand techniques. Again, there is no substitute for repetition. Free-sparring practice, by comparison, may be more exciting than standing in various stances practicing basic strikes and punches. However, the ability to deliver such a punch or strike and finish the opponent with one blow will not come as the result of free-sparring practice; rather, it will be the result of countless thousands of repetitions of the punch, including many against the striking-post to improve focus. In like manner, it will be impossible to take advantage of an opening in the opponent's defenses if the ability to adjust the distance between the two fighters is nonexistent. This is learned through continual basic practice in stepping, which will allow the fighter to develop the ability to move forward on the attack or retreat on the defensive as the situation requires.

It has often been said that karate fighting begins with a strong defense. The basic philosophy of many of the major karate schools is that a strong defense will prevent further attack. An opponent whose kick is blocked by a powerful downward block that raises a lump on his shin bone will feel the pain and be reluctant to attempt another kick. This is what is meant by winning while being on the defensive. If the block is strong enough, the attacker will be so intimidated that he will be afraid to attack further. Many traditional schools of karate have their students train their blocking arms by blocking against each other, in order to toughen the forearms and make them resistant to pain. This gives the fighter confidence that a block will be so strong that the opponent will think twice before attacking again.

Speed in technique is the direct result of repetition. Although some people are naturally faster than others, excellent improvement in speed is developed via muscle memory through the continuous practice of individual techniques. While this type of training may bore some, it is the only way to increase speed. Those who wish to have speed in their techniques must not begin by attempting to go fast before absolutely correct movement in the technique has been achieved. Once the movement is correct, the speed will come naturally as practice continues. If the form of the technique is incorrect, then there will be limits on the speed that a practitioner may obtain.

Correct timing is the result of basic training in the sparring drills. Through various types of sparring drills such as one-attack or three-attack, basic timing for the punch and kick are learned. If the fighter's timing is off, he will find it impossible to respond correctly to an attack and may deliver the technique too soon or too late for it to be effective. Also, by practicing the basic drills a fighter will have time to observe the movement of various opponents as they initiate different types of attacks. In free-sparring, things happen too quickly for any real training to take place. Free-sparring is simply the combined application of all the basic elements of fighting. Experience in these elements will give the fighter the ability to face different opponents in diverse situations. Such experience may be the result of training in the basic elements and also the result of training in actual free-sparring.

Which techniques to use and how to use them properly must be determined by adapting them to the individual's own body and its natural movement. Techniques that are counter to the natural movement of the body are difficult to perform and at best are a waste of time and energy. If executed incorrectly in the course of combat, they may be quite costly.

The admonition here is clear, those who wish to attain proficiency in fighting must first build a strong base of support through the practice of basic techniques. To practice in any other way will severely limit the future progress of the karate practitioner.

The Foundations of Advanced Technique

Karate is very similar to other athletic endeavors in that intensive training in basic movements is necessary in order to produce superior advanced techniques. The general advice to all beginners and intermediate trainees is to concentrate heavily

Plate 7 Basic defensive movement consists of a number of elements, including blocking, body shifting, timing, and perception of attack.

on the basic kicks, punches, blocks, and stances so that perfect movement in each is accomplished. Once this has occurred, combinations of movements may be attempted and ultimately practiced against an opponent.

The pyramid chart below demonstrates the relationship between basic and advanced karate. Note that fighting ability, seen here as the ultimate goal of karate training in the physical sense, is based on a much greater proportion of repetitive movements in all the basic elements of fighting. Emphasis on repetition is essential in the earlier years of training. The second level of practice is the application of the techniques against an opponent, either real or imagined, through

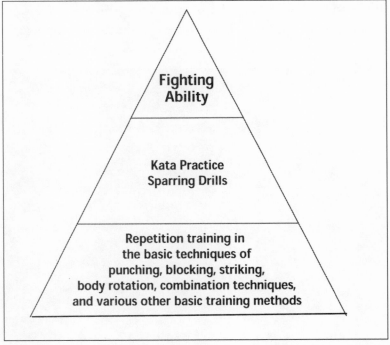

Plate 8 The relationship between basics, drills, kata, and fighting ability.

sparring drills and kata practice. All of these types of training lead to the ultimate physical goal, which is fighting ability.

In considering free-sparring practice, it is important to note that individuals will not be able to spar well if they cannot deliver a forceful, speedy blow to their opponent. Neither will their defense be effective if they have not trained intensively in well-balanced shifting movements. This type of training is essential if superior sparring ability is desired.

Those trainees who attempt to free-spar too soon and too often at the expense of basic practice will quickly develop a fighting sense. However, after some initial moves of defense and attack are developed, they will be unable to progress at a satisfactory rate, and their development of technique will be less than if they had mastered the basics first. Human beings first learn to crawl, then to stand and walk, and finally to run and perform athletic exercises. This pattern of development is normal, and the child who tries to run before learning to walk usually falls down. It is far better to build a solid foundation on which to base later advanced techniques.

This sequence of training, however, is not popular. Beginners who start karate training in order to learn how to fight, frequently fail to see the connection between basic drills and fighting, or between kata and actual fighting ability. This is a problem that karate instructors must address. They must educate their students as to the importance of basic practice. Following this method, they will produce students with superior technique and fighting ability.

Basic Defense

Basic defensive movement consists of three separate motions: hand and arm movement, body rotation, and body shifting.

Figure 1

Figure 2

Figure 3

Figure 4

Figure 5

Figure 6

Figure 7

Figure 8

Figure 9

In the performance of a normal karate block, all three are performed together, although there are times when it may be possible to defend oneself by using only one motion.

Hand and arm movements are commonly used in blocks. Shown in Figures 1 and 2 is the outside forearm block. This movement is usually performed as a defense against a punching or kicking attack to the midsection of the body.

Body rotation is necessary as well, in order to present less of a target area to the opponent (Figs. 3–4). It is natural to rotate the body in many of the blocks, since the blocking movement of the arm generates a turning movement of the body, along with that generated by the rotation of the hips.

In addition to rotating the body and moving the arm, it is necessary to shift the body backward to increase distance between yourself and your attacker (Figs. 5–6).

Normal blocking techniques include all three of the motions, performed simultaneously. Figures 7 through 10 show the outside forearm block performed in a front stance. The performer begins in the natural stance and begins the block by raising his left arm high to his left side (Figs. 7–8). He then steps back with his right foot, into the left front stance, simultaneously rotating his body and finishing the block (Figs. 9–10).

Figure 10

Figure 11

Figure 12

Figure 13

Figure 14

Figure 15

Figure 16

Against an opponent, simply performing the arm movement may not successfully block the punch (Fig. 11). Rotation of the body helps to deflect the movement (Fig. 12). In some cases, it may be possible to simply avoid the blow by rotating the body (Fig. 13) or shifting (Fig. 14). The best and most inclusive move for defense, however, combines all three motions (Fig. 15). In basic training, therefore, it is best if students practice their blocks using body rotation and shifting movements whenever possible.

Distancing

One of the most important elements in fighting is distancing. In competition, one of the main reasons that contestants fail to score with techniques is incorrect distance. Simply put, distancing means the proper relationship between the combatants in order for one of them to deliver a strong technique.

To demonstrate this principle, let us examine the photos. In Figures 16 and 17 the attacker attempts a jab to his adversary's face. However, he is too far away, and his punch falls short (Fig. 17). In Figure 18 he is a bit too close and his technique, while making contact, does not develop full power. In competition,

Figure 17

Figure 18

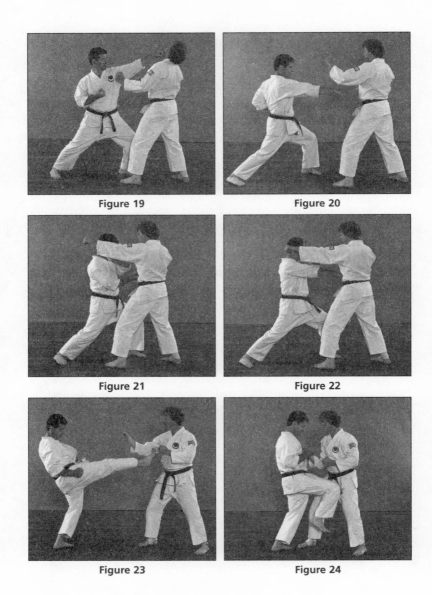

Figure 19

Figure 20

Figure 21

Figure 22

Figure 23

Figure 24

this might be scored as a half-point. In actual combat, it may not be enough to finish his opponent and may put his own life in jeopardy. Figure 19 demonstrates the correct distance.

In Figures 20 through 22 the counterpunch is depicted. Figure 20 demonstrates an attempted punch at too great a distance — it simply does not make contact — while in Figure 21 the distance is too close, making it necessary to deliver a punch at less than full power. In the case of Figure 20, the attacker should either have shifted forward slightly to close the distance, or perhaps shift-stepped and kicked, since there is almost sufficient distance. An alternative to the short punch in Figure 21 might have been an elbow strike, a technique that would have been more effective, since the point of the elbow would have traveled a longer distance to the target and thus would have developed more power. Figure 22 shows the correct distance for the punch.

Powerful kicking techniques also require correct distancing. In Figure 23, the kick is delivered from too great a distance and does not reach the opponent, while in Figure 24 the kick is jammed since the kicker is too close to his opponent. In this case a knee kick might have been more practical. Figure 25 demonstrates correct distancing, with the leg almost fully extended and enough power left to deliver a strong blow against the opponent.

Figure 25

As basic demonstrations of distance, the figures above illustrate the point. However, in all cases the opponent has not moved. The attacker may find that his opponent moves forward or backward as he executes a technique, thereby causing the distance to be incorrect. In such cases, it is necessary to make instant adjustments by foot or hip shifting. Naturally, the ability to do so depends on the length and quality of the performer's training.

Plate 9   An essential fighting skill to master is the correct use of distancing. Here the elbow strike is demonstrated as a short-range attacking technique.

Timing

One of the most important elements of fighting is timing. Without proper timing, defense is impossible. As it relates to fighting, timing simply means applying the block or attack at the proper moment in order to avoid being hit, or in order to allow you to hit your opponent. The figures below demonstrate how timing works.

In the execution of a simple rising block, used here against a punch to the face, the defender will be hit if his block is too late (Fig. 26). Completing the block after the punch (Fig. 27) is useless, since he has already been hit. In like manner, executing a block too soon (Fig. 28) will ensure that he will be hit, since his blocking arm will move too soon and miss the punch (Fig. 29).

The same attention to timing must be followed in defending against kicks. If timing is incorrect and too late, the kick will score (Figs. 30–31). If the block is begun too early, the blocking arm will have passed its effective point, and the kick will score after the arm has passed by (Figs. 32–33).

Figure 26　　　　**Figure 27**

Figure 28　　　　**Figure 29**

Figure 30

Figure 31

Figure 32

Figure 33

Figure 34

Figure 35

On a more advanced level, fighters try to anticipate their attackers' moves. In order to do this successfully a great deal of training in basic sparring drills is necessary. In figure 34 two fighters face each other in sparring stances. Figure 35 shows the fighter on the right initiating a punching attack by stepping forward with his right foot and attempting a right punch to the face. The fighter on the left has anticipated his move, but his timing is off and he executes a right counterpunch too soon, terminating the technique before his attacker is in range. This opens him to attack. Had he waited a split second longer, he would have caught his opponent at the right moment, just before he was able to complete his technique. Figure 36 demonstrates correct timing.

The ability to correctly time movements against an opponent is not something that a fighter develops and may then set aside while practicing other techniques. Timing must be continually reinforced through practice, otherwise it is lost. This may be accomplished through continual repetition of the basic sparring drills, as well as the more advanced sparring drills for accomplished karate practitioners. It is often said that once an individual has stopped training, the first thing to go is timing. Experience has proven this to be true.

Figure 36

Speed

It might be expected that there are some specific drills that will enhance speed. Actually, this is not the case. Speed is a natural development of repetitive movement. As the body becomes accustomed to the karate movement, that movement is performed in a more relaxed state, conserving more energy. This allows the punch or kick to be executed with maximum speed.

In order to build speed in a technique, it is necessary that the basic movements be perfected. In the case of the counter-punch, for instance, incorrect body posture, stance, or hip position may make it impossible to deliver the technique correctly. Beginners should concentrate on making the technique as correct as possible in the earlier phases of training. Those who attempt maximum speed at first will never have correct movement and therefore will be hampered in their attempt to develop their potential speed. Once a movement has been developed correctly, speed will be a natural result of repetition training via muscle memory.

Some methods of training for speed involve punching or kicking several hundred times without stopping. As muscle fatigue begins to set in, it will not be possible for the trainee to kick with force, and he will have to kick or punch using technique. This type of training will build endurance as well as speed in individual technique.

Hip Shifting

Since basically all major body movements begin with the hips, a thorough understanding of how they affect movement is necessary. As discussed in the section on natural body movement, it is necessary to move the hips prior to initiating leg and foot action. This being the case, it is desirable to train the hip to move more rapidly in karate movements in order to facilitate techniques of attack and defense. Depicted herein are several drills designed to enhance hip movement.

Figures 37–39 demonstrate a basic method of utilizing the hip in order to evade an attack and institute a counterattack. In Figure 37 the model is in the left front stance, having just completed a punch with the left hand. In response to an approaching adversary, he shifts the left foot rapidly back to the right (Fig. 38) and then steps in with the right foot, executing a right lunge punch (Fig. 39). This movement should be practiced through numerous repetitions, shifting first the right

side and then the left, in place. Note that the hip must remain at the original level; to raise and lower it in this movement will slow the performer down and unbalance him. In like manner, the back must be kept straight, in order to facilitate movement.

Figure 37

Figure 38

Figure 39

Figure 40

Figure 41

Figure 42

Figure 43

If the performer were to lean forward, he would lose the ability to shift at maximum speed, since his hips would tilt back and be contrary to his natural body position.

Another necessary movement from the standpoint of sparring is the ability to evade a blow and swiftly counterattack. This may be accomplished by slightly shifting the entire body to the rear and then back in toward the opponent. This type of movement is demonstrated in Figures 40 through 43. The performer has just completed a counterpunch (Fig. 40). He crosses his hands to perform the downward block (Fig. 41). As the block is executed, the entire body is shifted backward, approximately 12 inches (Fig. 42). Note that the relative foot position is not changed and that the hips have not been raised. This type of movement must be accomplished without "hopping," and the body must be kept as near level as possible. The rear leg is cocked slightly in order to provide thrust for the forward movement. As the rear foot is thrust against the floor, it provides drive to shift the entire body forward approximately 12 inches as the performer completes a counterpunch (Fig. 43). This should be practiced first as a single movement back and a single movement forward, and then the shift back and forward together.

Still another training method for hip shifting is shown in Figures 44 through 48. The performer adopts a front stance with the hands raised in sparring position (Fig. 44). Without raising the hips or moving the body upward, the feet are simply switched, with the lead foot moving forward as the front foot moves backward. It is difficult to do this without raising

Figure 44   Figure 45

Figure 46   Figure 47

Figure 48

the body in a "hopping" movement. However it is necessary to do so. The performer then switches foot positions again (Fig. 46) and then counterpunches with the right hand (Fig. 47). He then resumes the ready position (Fig. 48). It is usually best to practice three switches and then punch, since this gives punching practice on both sides.

Stance Shift

Many subtle movements in fighting are based on a thorough understanding of simple techniques. In the course of training, it is usually a part of basic practice to shift from one stance to another, and beginners frequently fail to see the need for such drills. However, they do have a practical use in combat situations.

Depicted here is the basic shift in stance from front to back stance. In Figure 49 the defender on the left faces his opponent in the front stance. The attacker has punched with his right hand in order to demonstrate that he is at correct distance for the technique to make contact. Without moving his feet, the defender simply shifts into the back stance (Fig. 50). Note that this subtle shift in stance has placed his face and

Figure 49   **Figure 50**

Figure 51

Figure 52

Figure 53

Figure 54

Figure 55

body out of range of his opponent's punching hand. He would then be able to shift back into the front stance and deliver a counterpunch with his right hand.

In Figures 51 through 53 the defender has not changed stance. Rather than shift into a back stance, he has simply leaned his upper body away from the punch (Fig. 52) and then using the movement of his hip combined with his upper body, leaned forward to adjust the range for his own right-handed counterattack (Fig. 53).

Such subtleties in movement are usually practiced in basic training; however, many students fail to realize their usefulness in actual fighting situations.

Linear Movement

In the performance of karate techniques there are two basic types of movement that the practitioner must master: linear and circular. Although it is frequently said that linear movements are used primarily for attack and circular movements primarily for defense, this is not necessarily a hard and fast rule, as either may be used for attack or defense.

Linear movement basically indicates a movement in a straight line, either toward or away from an opponent. Thus, on the attack, the linear path leads straight to the opponent, or, if the opponent attacks, the linear path leads directly away from him. In Figures 54 and 55 are depicted the most common form of linear movement, the simple step backward to perform a blocking technique. In a case of this sort, it is necessary to follow rapidly with a counterpunch or kick, in order to stop the opponent's attack. Mastery of this type of movement is facilitated by continued drilling in the pattern of moving forward and backward while in stance and drilling in the performance of techniques.

Figure 56

Figure 57

Figure 58

Figure 59

Figure 60

Figure 61

A basic drill for stepping backward and then forward in a linear movement is shown in Figures 56 through 60. The beginning position is the right sparring stance (Fig. 56). The performer steps directly backward and uses the left hand to jab to the face (Fig. 57) in combination with a right counterpunch (Fig. 58). He then moves forward, executing a right front kick (Fig. 59) and, as his foot lands, follows with a left counterpunch (Fig. 60).

Figures 61 through 69 demonstrate still another of many possible drills for attaining proficiency in linear movement. In Figure 61 the performer assumes the sparring stance with the left foot forward. He shifts the left foot forward and jabs to the face with the left hand (Fig. 62). He then steps forward

Figure 62   Figure 63

Figure 64   Figure 65

Figure 66

Figure 67

Figure 68

Figure 69

Figure 70

Figure 71

and executes a lunge punch to the face (Fig. 63) combined with a counterpunch to the midsection (Fig. 64). The right sparring stance is then taken (Fig. 65). Shifting the left foot backward, the performer jabs to the face with the right hand (Fig. 66). He then steps backward with the right foot and executes first a left jab to the face (Fig. 67) and then a right counterpunch to the midsection (Fig. 68). From there he assumes the left sparring stance (Fig. 69) in preparation for the next repetition of the drill. This particular drill works well as a two-person drill, with one side retreating as the other advances. The movement is then reversed.

Figures 70 through 73 demonstrate a combination of kicking and punching movements, all on a linear pattern. Begin in a left front stance (Fig. 70). Step forward and execute a right front snap-kick (Fig. 71). Step down with your right foot into the front stance and then execute a left side thrust-kick (Figs. 72–73). Step down into the left front stance and then execute a right roundhouse kick (Figs. 74–75). As your right foot

Figure 72   **Figure 73**

Figure 74   **Figure 75**

Figure 76   **Figure 77**

comes down in a front stance, execute a right back-fist strike to the face (Fig. 76) and then a left counterpunch to the mid-section (Fig. 77).

In addition to giving basic training in linear movement, these drills also provide excellent practice in body shifting and combination techniques.

Circular Movement

Circular movement involves pivoting the body around a particular point and is thought to be of greatest use in avoiding an attack. While this is true, there are also applications for initiating an attack and counterattacking.

Figures 78 through 80 show the most common, basic movement following the circular pattern. In this case, the performer has swung his rear leg across approximately 45 degrees, turning his body and avoiding the attack by use of a forearm block. This places him at the side of the opponent, who then has to change

Figure 78

Figure 79

Figure 80

Figure 81

Figure 82

Figure 83

Figure 84

Figure 85

Figure 86

direction in order to pursue him. It is also possible to get completely to the side of the opponent by swinging the leg closer to 90 degrees, as shown in Figures 81 and 82. The performer has blocked a hand technique with his left hand and follows with a right counterpunch (Fig. 83).

A greater degree of turn is also possible, as shown in Figures 84 through 87. Here the performer has evaded a kick by use of a sweeping downward block (Fig. 85) as he turns his entire body in a clockwise movement, swinging his right foot around into the front stance and accomplishing a turn of about 135 degrees (Fig. 88). He then counters his opponent with a right counterpunch (Fig. 87).

A valuable drill for practicing circular movement is shown in Figures 88 through 92. The performer adopts the sparring stance with the left foot forward (Fig. 88). He shifts into the front stance and executes a right counterpunch to the midsection (Fig. 89). Immediately after completing the right punch, he pivots his body 90 degrees on his left foot in a

Figure 87

Figure 88

Figure 89

Figure 90

Figure 91

Figure 92

Figure 93

Figure 94

clockwise movement (Fig. 90) and, as he places his foot down in back of him, executes a left punch to the face and a right counterpunch to the midsection (Figs. 91–92).

It is not necessary to use only a front stance in circular movement, because any stance is suitable. Figures 93 through 96 show the *sanchin* stance used in the same circular manner, along with a circular block. As the hands negate the attacker's punching technique, the rear foot moves clockwise, rotating the body around the pivot point and placing the defender to the side of his attacker (Fig. 96), where he may use whatever counterattack is necessary.

Combined Linear and Circular Movement

Practical considerations in combat dictate that one should never settle into patterns of movement, lest the opponent observe them and be able to devise an appropriate strategy for countering. Accordingly, simply to adopt linear movement as

Figure 95   **Figure 96**

Figure 97   Figure 98   Figure 99

Figure 100   Figure 101   Figure 102

Figure 103   Figure 104   Figure 105

the mode of attack and circular movement as the means of defense makes no sense; rather, it is more practical to combine both types of movement whenever necessary to defeat an opponent. In short, whatever is workable should be utilized, since there are no rules in combat. Demonstrated here is an application of both circular and linear movement, combining the extended knife-hand block, the roundhouse kick, and both linear and circular movement in the front stance.

The performer begins in a natural stance, the weight evenly distributed on both feet (Fig. 97). He steps back with his right foot into the front stance, using his right hand to block a punch with the extended knife-hand block (Fig. 98). Pulling his opponent's arm forward, he executes a roundhouse kick and then instead of stepping directly forward, he steps across at about a 45-degree angle with his right foot (Figs. 99–101). Using a counterclockwise turn of the body, he sweeps his left leg around into a front stance, simultaneously using the left extended knife-hand block (Figs. 102–103). Once in position, he is able to repeat the drill in the opposite direction, using a left roundhouse kick and then stepping across, rather than straight ahead, completing a circular movement by sweeping the right leg around in a clockwise

Figure 106   **Figure 107**   **Figure 108**

Figure 109   Figure 110   Figure 111

Figure 112   Figure 113   Figure 114

Figure 115   Figure 116   Figure 117

turn and again blocking (Figs. 104–108). This has placed the performer back in the beginning position, and the drill may be repeated.

Figures 109 through 118 demonstrate still another combination of linear and circular movements. The performer begins in the left front stance (Fig. 109). He shifts his weight to his left foot and executes a right front snap-kick (Fig. 110). He then steps down with his right foot into the right front stance (Fig. 111). Then he pivots on his right foot 90 degrees in a clockwise

movement and raises his left leg high to the side in preparation for a left roundhouse kick (Fig. 112). He executes a left roundhouse kick and then steps down into a left front stance (Figs. 113–114) and executes a right counterpunch (Fig. 115). He pivots 90 degrees in a counterclockwise movement on his left foot (Figs. 116–117), executing a left downward block as he assumes the left front

Figure 118

stance and counterpunches with his right hand (Fig. 118).

CHAPTER FOUR

Strategy

Plate 10   *Karate Ni Sente Nashi.* (In Karate There Is No First Attack). Calligraphy by Master Masatoshi Nakayama.

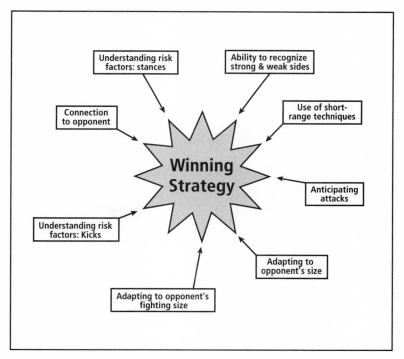

Plate 11 The elements of winning strategy.

Figure 1

Figure 2

Figure 3

Risk Factors: Stances

Since karate is basically self-defense it follows that whatever movements are executed should be done in light of their direct application to self-protection. Accordingly, there are movements and positions that carry greater or lesser risk to the participant. The safest course of action obviously, would be to utilize those techniques that present the least risk to the karate practitioner; however, it is not always possible to use such techniques. Nevertheless, in most cases, common sense would rule that a technique with less of a risk factor would be best to use. Those techniques that carry a higher risk factor require more skill to execute successfully. Therefore, use of such high risk moves requires greater practice. Let us examine some of the basic stances and kicks to determine which pose a greater or lesser threat to the performer's safety.

Stances

Demonstrated in Figures 1 through 11 are various movements performed using the front stance (*zenkutsu-dachi*). This is probably the safest method of facing the opponent. It will be observed that both feet face toward the opponent and the weight is evenly distributed. The stance is modified from basic front stance by shortening it slightly in order to facilitate rapid movement. In this position it is possible to block an opponent's attack, since both hands are in front of the body. In Figures 2 and 3 the attacker has executed a left jab to the face, and the defender is easily able to deflect the punch with a left forearm block and respond with a strong counterpunch

Figure 4

Figure 5

Figure 6

to the midsection. It is also a relatively simple matter for the defender to launch a hand attack against his opponent, since he faces him directly.

Figures 4 and 5 show the model on the left initiating an attack with the front kick. This is a simple maneuver in this stance since the body faces directly forward. It is also possible to initiate an attack using the front foot, in this case a roundhouse kick, as shown in Figures 6 and 7. Kicking with either

Figure 7

Figure 8

Figure 9

Figure 10

Figure 11

the front or rear leg is not difficult because the opponent is directly in front.

It is also possible to use the side thrust-kick, demonstrated in Figures 8 and 9. The back kicks, either thrust or round-house, may be executed by pivoting on the lead foot (Figs. 10–11). Because with the front stance it is possible to execute a myriad of attacks easily and to defend against attacks, this stance has the lowest risk factor of all the stances utilized in karate. In addition, the placement of the feet makes it possible to move quickly forward and backward, as well as from side to side, utilizing either circular or linear movements.

Several other stances share the properties of the front stance, including s*ochin-dachi* (rooted stance), *sanchin-dachi* (hourglass stance), and *hangetsu-dachi* (crescent stance). Both sochin-dachi and hangetsu-dachi may be seen as variations on the front stance, since the feet and body face toward the opponent, making use of both hands for attack and defense possible. In the case of sochin-dachi, the main difference between it and the front stance is that it is very low and designed to resist an opponent's attack. Its low posture makes it less maneuverable than a front stance. This is also the case with hangetsu-dachi, since the inward tension of the legs makes rapid movement more difficult. Sanchin-dachi also shares this inward tension aspect, and a practitioner using an inward tension stance is not able to move as well. Generally, these three stances are used more for defense than attack, since their characteristics do not allow maximum, rapid movement. Therefore, they fall into the category of having a

Figure 12

Figure 13

Figure 14

medium risk factor, since they are good defensive postures, but lack the mobility of some of the other stances.

The straddle stance (*kiba-dachi*) carries a higher risk factor both in its offensive and defensive uses. This is primarily because one hand is close to the opponent, while the rear hand is far away, with the hip turned, making blocking and counterattacking difficult with that hand. Kicking techniques are possible with the straddle stance; however, they are somewhat limited. The front leg may be used for side or roundhouse kicks; however, in order to use the rear leg the hips must be turned forward, telegraphing the move to the opponent. It is possible to use the turning back kicks more effectively, since the body is already half turned. In short, this position is usable, but not as safe as the front stance. As shown in Figures 12 through 14, the model on the right stands in the straddle stance, with his left knee near his opponent. Since the side of the knee is a target area, it is vulnerable to attack using a thrusting kick, as shown in Figure 13. This forces the defender around and allows an attack to his kidney area. The use of the straddle stance also exposes one to various sweeping and turning movements (Figs. 15–19). In this case, the lead leg is swept upward, turning the defender and exposing

Figure 15

Figure 16

Figure 17

Figure 18

his back to attack. Use of the straddle stance may be desirable at times; however, the risks associated with it should be considered in formulating a fighting strategy.

Still another stance with a higher risk factor than the front stance is the cat-foot stance (*neko-ashi-dachi*). The best use of this stance involves quickly shifting into and out of it, since most of the weight is carried on the rear leg. Although this facilitates kicking with the forward leg, the rear leg is useless for kicking, since it must support the body. As demonstrated in Figures 20 and 21, it is possible to jam the opponent's kick and throw him down, since he has little mobility in this position. As with the front stance, the hands are generally in front of the body, making hand movements easier, but the unbalanced position of the body makes their use weak and ineffective. Only movements using little power, such as spear-hand attacks to the eyes, would be effective.

Another basic stance is the back stance (*kokutsu-dachi*). It is used primarily as an intermediate position, while dodging an

Figure 19

Figure 20

Figure 21

Figure 22

attack and preparing for movement back toward the opponent. Since only about 30 percent of the body weight is carried on the front leg, it is easily swept from the inside (Figs. 22–24) or the outside, opening the user to attack as shown.

The problem of which stance to use in free-fighting, then, must be decided by an examination of the risk factors inherent in each. The front stance affords the most mobility, protection, and ability to use varied techniques. This is probably because it most closely approaches the natural movement of the body, facing toward the attacker. Such considerations, however, presuppose a single attacker approaching from the front. In cases where a second attacker approaches from the side, it may be necessary to utilize a straddle stance in order to

Figure 23

Figure 24

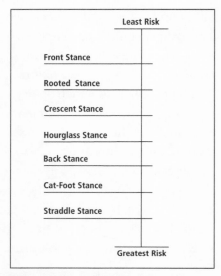

Least Risk

Front Stance

Rooted Stance

Crescent Stance

Hourglass Stance

Back Stance

Cat-Foot Stance

Straddle Stance

Greatest Risk

Plate 12 Risk factors of the various stances.

Plate 13 High roundhouse kicks have a moderate risk factor. Even though the kick exposes the attacker to a counter, he is facing the opponent and still able to defend himself.

move sideways toward that attack and execute a side kick. Back stances are used primarily to dodge an attack and move back into the opponent with a countering technique. Cat-foot stances are useful in certain situations where the opponent's attack is short and a front-leg kick is desirable. In short, all stances are useful, but the determination of which to use depends on circumstance, with an underlying understanding of the strengths and weaknesses of each. The chart on page 104 shows the degree of risk associated with the different stances.

Risk Factors: Kicks

The use of kicking techniques places the kicker in a precarious position, since all the weight of the body is placed on the supporting leg. Hands may be used in an attack without seriously jeopardizing balance and position; however, the use of the legs is an entirely different matter, since a blocked or caught leg may be used to turn the kicker's body or throw him to the ground. It follows, therefore, that the use of such kicking techniques carries more inherent risk to the kicker than do hand techniques. In like manner, some kicks carry a greater risk factor than others. The choice of which to use must, in many cases, be determined by the abilities of the performer and the particular situation. An examination of the more common kicks will demonstrate which carry greater or lesser risks to the user.

Front Kick

The kick with the lowest risk factor to the performer is the front kick. This is because the performance of the front kick requires that the body directly face the opponent, allowing free use of the hands for follow-up attacks or blocks. Using

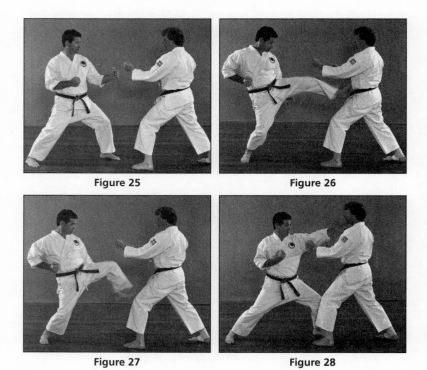

Figure 25   **Figure 26**

Figure 27   **Figure 28**

the front kick with the lead leg carries less of a risk than performing it with the back leg, since the body generally remains in place and is easy to control. Shown here (Figs. 25–28) is the front kick to the stomach using the lead leg. As the kick is withdrawn, the left hand easily performs a punch to the face. Even if the defender blocks the kick and turns the kicker slightly (Figs. 29–30), it is still possible to complete the follow- up punch to the face.

Figure 29

Figure 30

Figure 31

Figure 32

Figure 33

When kicking with the back leg, the body must move forward toward the opponent. This generates greater power and requires more of a commitment on the part of the attacker (Figs. 31–33). It is still possible to follow with a punch to the face when the kick is blocked (Figs. 34–36). Again, this is because the body is primarily facing to the front, allowing more of a defensive attitude.

Figure 34

Figure 35

Figure 36

Figure 37

Figure 38

Side Kicks

The side kick may be executed using the lead leg or the rear leg, depending on circumstances. As shown here (Figs. 37–38) it is performed using the rear leg. Note that the hips and body are turned to the side to utilize hip power in the kick. This side-facing position makes it difficult to block an opponent's counter if he blocks and turns the attacker (Figs. 39–42). The kick as shown was executed from the front stance; however, the results would be the same if the straddle stance were used, since the body would already be turned to the side.

Figure 39

Figure 40

Figure 41

Figure 42

Roundhouse Kicks

When executed with the front leg, the roundhouse kick has about the same risk factor as the front-leg front kick, since the body remains stationary and the hands are in front of the body ready to defend or follow with another technique. When the roundhouse kick is executed using the rear leg, a greater risk is presented (Figs. 43–44). The weight is shifted to the support leg and the kicking leg brought high to the side of the body. If the defender has good timing and steps forward, it is relatively easy to score with a punch to the midsection. This leaves the attacker injured and standing on one leg, a difficult situation from which to escape.

Figure 43

Figure 44

Back Kicks

From the standing position, the kick carrying the greatest risk is the back kick, with all its variations (hook, roundhouse, thrust, and snap). In order to perform this kick, the body must be turned so that the back is exposed to the defender. This makes any defense using the arms impossible. If the defender does not back up, but steps forward, he will easily score to the opponent's back (Figs. 45–47).

Figure 45

Figure 46

Figure 47

Figure 48

Figure 49

Jumping Kicks

Kicks that the performer leaves the floor to execute also carry a high risk. Once committed to the kick, there is no turning back until the feet land on the ground. Such kicks place the performer in a precarious position, since his balance may be upset while in the air, causing him to fall to the ground in a vulnerable position. To successfully execute a jumping kick requires more skill than executing a standing kick. Such kicks are primarily useful as a surprise move, since continued use of them in a fight may allow the opponent to exploit a moment of weakness.

Floor Kicks

Kicking at the opponent from the floor may be necessary, when one loses balance or is swept. On rare occasions, floor kicks may be used as a surprise attack; however, since the kicker surrenders mobility, they carry a great risk.

The roundhouse kick from the floor is useful primarily as one is thrown to the floor, because the opponent may be at close quarters and it is possible to score with it. As shown here (Figs. 48–49) it is easily blocked and countered with a side kick. Since the hands are used to support the body, it is not possible to use them effectively in defense.

Figure 50

Figure 51

Figure 52

Figure 53

Figure 54

Figure 55

A good self-defense move from the floor is the side thrust-kick to the knee. However, if the leg is blocked, the body is easily turned, allowing a follow-up punch to the body (Figs. 50–52). In like manner, the front kick from the floor (Figs. 53–55) may be blocked or evaded and countered with a kick. Most difficult of all kicks to execute successfully from the floor is the back thrust-kick (Figs. 56–58). With the back turned, it is difficult to see the opponent, much less score with the kick.

In summation, it may be observed that the floor kicking techniques are similar to the standing kicking techniques in that the kicks used facing the opponent present less risk than when the body is turned to the side or rear. The added factor

Figure 56

Figure 57

Figure 58

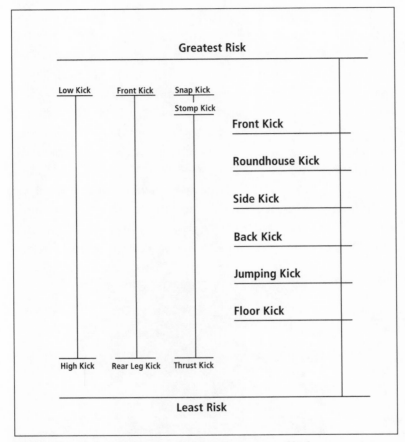

Plate 14 Risk factors associated with various types of kicks.

Figure 59

Figure 60

making floor kicks risky, however, is the lack of mobility on the part of the user and the inability to use the hands effectively. The various kicks, then, present different levels of risk to the user. This does not mean that one must use only the front-leg front kick in order to be safe. What it does imply is that in order to utilize all of the kicks effectively, it is necessary to be more skilled in those with higher risk factors. An opponent approaching from the side or rear may not allow the defender time to turn, and thus a side or back kick may be the safest response in that situation. As with all techniques, familiarity, skill, and common sense will dictate which is best to use in a given situation.

The chart on page 118 shows the relationship between kicks and their risk factors.

Strategy: Opponent's Size

In the course of regular karate training, sparring drills are practiced against a number of opponents. This allows the practitioner to become familiar with strategies against attackers of all sizes and physical abilities. Through this kind of training the student must develop the ability to determine an opponent's strong and weak points. Considered here is the element of size.

Two fighters face each other in left sparring stances (Fig. 59). The fighter on the left is about 6' 1" tall and weighs 195 pounds. The fighter on the right is 5' 6" tall and 165 pounds. Clearly the factor of strength and reach is in favor of the larger fighter. If the fighter on the right attempts a kicking attack, the fighter on the left has enough power to shift forward and block the attack, leaving the attacker open to a counterpunch (Fig. 60).

Figure 61

Figure 62

Figure 63

The larger fighter (left) can also outreach his opponent, as shown here. His arm is longer by several inches and as the fighter on the right steps forward, he cannot get close enough to complete his punch before he is countered (Figs. 61–62). This relative distance in arm length is shown in Figure 63.

The smaller fighter has an advantage in close-in fighting, since he needs less room to execute a technique with full power. As his opponent shifts forward and attempts a right counter-punch, he is able to dodge and counterattack with a right roundhouse elbow strike to the ribs (Figs. 64–65).

Figure 64

Figure 65

Figure 66

Figure 67

Figure 68

Figure 69

Figure 70

Figure 71

Figure 72

Figure 73

Still another defensive move for the smaller man involves slipping to the side so as to be out of the line of attack, thus negating his opponent's superior size (Figs. 66–67). In this case he retaliates with a right counterpunch to the ribs.

Shifting ability is usually an attribute of light and middleweight fighters. Here, the smaller man shifts backward to dodge a front kick (Figs. 68–69) and then counters with a right roundhouse kick as his opponent steps forward (Figs. 70–72). He then steps to the right side of his attacker (Fig. 73), pivots on his right foot, and delivers a right roundhouse kick to the back of his opponent's head (Figs. 74–75).

Understanding one's own strengths and weaknesses is vital to becoming a skilled fighter. Those who possess strength and power should train in techniques that maximize those attributes and avoid flashy movements that are more properly left to light and middleweight fighters. The latter must emphasize such shifting movements in their training, since they do not have the weight or reach to compete on other terms. Thus, light and middleweight fighters are well advised to spend a great deal of time on shifting and dodging movements, as well as combination techniques involving circular movements.

Figure 74

Figure 75

Figure 76   Figure 77

Figure 78   Figure 79

Figure 80   Figure 81

Figure 82

Strong and Weak Sides

A basic consideration when facing an opponent is how to move in order to avoid the opponent's strongest attack. Consequently, it is necessary to recognize that the opponent has a strong and a weak side. This means that the hand or foot on one side of the body is capable of delivering a stronger blow than those on the opposite side of the body. In general, this corresponds to the lead side and the rear side.

In Figure 76, the two combatants face one another. The attacker on the right shifts forward, executing a jab to the face. Sensing the attack, the defender shifts to the outside of his opponent (Fig. 77), blocking and countering with a punch to the side (Fig. 78). In so doing, the defender has moved to the weak side of his opponent, since the attacker cannot easily punch or kick at him with his left leg or arm.

In Figures 79 through 82, the defender has moved to the right, toward his attacker's strong side. Although he has blocked the attack (Fig. 80), he is in a position where the attacker can easily follow up his right-hand jab with a left counterpunch (Fig. 81). Even if the defender attempts to shift away, he is in position to be attacked by a front kick, as shown (Fig. 82). This is a basic tactical error, in that the defensive side has moved into a position on his opponent's strong side, giving him an advantage.

In sparring, therefore, it is necessary to move away from or to the outside of the opponent's lead foot. If the opponent leads with his left foot, then the defender should move to the right, and if the opponent has his right foot forward, then the defender should move to the left. As with all elements of strategy, this is a basic principle, but may have to be varied according to the situation.

Short-Range Techniques

As indicated in prior sections, it is desirable to distance one-self correctly from an opponent so as to deliver the strongest possible blow. This is not always possible, however, and in some cases the opponent may be too close to effectively utilize a long-range technique. In such cases, it may be necessary to use short-range techniques. Shown here are several examples of such techniques used against an opponent.

Plate 15 The use of short-range techniques is frequently necessary. Here the defender uses a combination of a hooking wrist block and a palm-heel strike.

Drill 1

In this situation (Figs. 83–85) the opponent has stepped in and attacked with a lunge punch to the face. The defensive side has blocked by shifting forward and thrusting his palm-heel against the attacker's shoulder, unbalancing him (Fig. 84). He then follows through with a rising elbow strike (Fig. 85). Although he is close to his opponent, the striking part of the elbow has developed power since it has traveled a fairly long distance on its circular path to the target.

Figure 83

Figure 84

Figure 85

Figure 86

Figure 87

Figure 88

Drill 2

Here the use of the outside forearm block is coupled with a roundhouse elbow strike to the side (Figs. 86–88) . Again the point of the elbow has traveled a good distance to the target, following a circular path and developing power.

Figure 89

Figure 90

Figure 91

Drill 3

Punches may also be used as blocks or stopping techniques. Here (Figs. 89–91) the defender steps to his attacker's strong side and blocks the punch with his left upper arm as he simultaneously strikes the opponent's chin with a punch. He follows with a close punch to the solar plexus. In this case power is developed by shifting the body forward in the direction of the punch (Fig. 91).

Figure 92

Figure 93

Figure 94

Drill 4

The knife-hand strike may be used either close in or at medium range. As the attacker punches to the face (Figs. 92–94), the defender blocks with an extended knife-hand block (Fig. 93), following with a knife-hand strike to the neck (Fig. 94).

Connection

One of the essential elements of fighting is connection to one's opponent. Simply put, this implies maintaining the correct spatial relationship with the opponent, so that you are always at the correct distance to counterattack or initiate an attack. There are numerous methods of practicing this, including the basic drills of three-attack and five-attack sparring. In practicing these drills, it is necessary to make sure that during each step the correct distance is maintained for the counterpunch. This may seem to be the same as simple distancing, and indeed, the two are interrelated, but connection implies a continuous relationship, whereas distancing may be practiced just when one is ready for the counterattack.

Still another method of practicing connection is to have an opponent execute continuous attacks toward you, utilizing linear movement. As your opponent does this, simply shift backward continually while keeping appropriate distance for a counterpunch. This type of practice will then allow proper connection to be maintained in free-fighting.

Figure 95

Figure 96

Figure 97

Figure 98

Anticipating Attacks

One of the best methods of scoring against the opponent is to attack him at a moment when he is unable to defend. This type of opening is what the skilled fighter looks for; however, it is difficult to perceive unless a great deal of training has been accomplished.

It is relatively simple to devise a countermove against an opponent if you know what that opponent is going to do. However, this is not always possible. What may be determined more easily, is the moment when the opponent launches an attack. Since few fighters are able to move forward into the attack without in some way telegraphing the move, an astute observer will be able to perceive the initiation of an attack. Through continuous repetition in basic drills involving forward shifting, it is possible to catch the opponent as he is moving forward, preferably as his feet are nearly in line. If the defender shifts forward and jabs or counterpunches he will be able to score easily on the opponent, who will not be in a good position to defend himself.

Demonstrated here are two basic shifts involving an anticipation of the attack. In Figures 95 and 96 the attacker on the right has begun his forward movement, either to punch or kick. Rather than shifting sideways or backward to avoid the attack, the defender on the left has shifted his left foot forward and jabbed to his opponent's chin, catching him as he moves forward. The force of both bodies moving together makes this a very powerful technique.

In Figures 97 and 98 the attacker on the right has begun to kick with his right leg. Rather than shift backward and allow his attacker room to kick, the defender on the left shifts his entire body forward several inches and delivers a counterpunch to his attacker's midsection, catching him just as his

Figure 99

Figure 100

Figure 101

foot leaves the ground. In this position, the attacker is basically defenseless and has been effectively countered.

In order to execute this type of movement it is necessary for
the defensive side to observe the opponent's movements care-
fully so as to catch him just as he begins his attack. This principle is frequently referred to as *sen no sen*, a Japanese term
indicating that one has seized the initiative first. In practical
terms, the defender on the left has actually attacked first, by
waiting for an opening in his opponent's defense. Although
the attacker seems to have initiated movement first, the
defender has seized the initiative from him and scored by
beating him to the punch.

Figures 99 through 101 demonstrate a method of taking
the initiative away from the opponent. The attacker (right)
begins to step forward (Fig. 99). Sensing his movement, the
defender (left) steps forward with his right foot and blocks
down with his left hand, stopping his opponent's attack (Fig.
100). He immediately follows with a lunge punch to the midsection (Fig. 101).

Figures 102 and 103 demonstrate a method of stopping an opponent's kicking attack. The attacker (right) raises his knee to kick and as he does this, the defender steps forward, simultaneously blocking down with his left hand and attacking his opponent's face with his right fist, stopping the attack while the opponent is off balance (Fig. 103)

Figure 102

Figure 103

CHAPTER FIVE

Sparring Drills

Since the purpose of physical training in karate includes the ability to defend oneself, it is necessary to practice various movements of attack and defense against an opponent. Only in this manner can one learn the proper application of blocks and counters to an opponent's attacks. Fighting consists of a number of constituent elements, and in order to perfect fighting technique one must practice drills that develop skill in each of the elements. This is why there are so many different sparring drills, ranging from prearranged sparring to free-fighting.

The drills presented here are representative of the types of training that are necessary to produce complete mastery of fighting technique; however, they are by no means exhaustive. Listed below are the basic elements of fighting and the drills that prove useful in developing each. Needless to say, each drill has a relationship to sparring ability; however, some drills are better for training in one specific element than in others.

Basic Defense: three-attack sparring, five-attack sparring, one-attack sparring

Distancing: three-attack sparring, five-attack sparring, semifree-sparring

Timing: one-attack sparring, semifree-sparring

Speed: one-attack sparring, semifree-sparring, free-sparring

Hip Shifting: one-attack sparring, semifree-sparring, hip-shifting drills

Linear Movement: three-attack sparring, five-attack sparring

Plate 16 The author and Frank Woon-a-Tai, Chief Instructor of the ISKF Canada Federation, practice a direction-reversing drill under the watchful eye of Master Masatoshi Nakayama, as Master Teruyuki Okazaki looks on.

Circular Movement: one-attack sparring,
    semifree-sparring, slow-motion free-sparring

Combined Linear and Circular Movement:
    Semifree-sparring, slow-motion free-sparring

Stance Shifting: one-attack sparring, semifree-
    sparring

Strong Side-Weak Side: slow-motion free-sparring,
    free-sparring

The drills listed here are suggested to provide a means for the improvement of particular elements of sparring. For instance, if in the course of free-sparring it is found that one's opponent seems to be frequently out of range, then additional practice of three- or five-attack sparring, or even semifree-sparring, would be helpful. In discovering a weak point in one's technique, it is necessary to isolate that element from the other elements of fighting and work on it intensively, gradually integrating that element back into free-sparring. Simply continuing to free-spar will not give enough practice in that particular skill. However, drilling with the weakness in mind will ensure that overall fighting ability will be improved.

Three-Attack Sparring

Three-attack sparring *(sanbon kumite)* is one of the basic methods of training the skills of shifting, blocking, and distancing. It should be practiced against a number of different individuals in order to allow the widest range of experience.

The first set of drills involves hand attacks to the face, midsection, and lower sections.

Figure 1

Figure 2

Figure 3

Drill 1 (Figs. 1–5)

After the students bow to each other, the attacker steps back with his right foot and executes a left downward block (Fig. 1). His opponent remains in the natural stance. It is necessary to practice defense this way because this is the natural position of the body, and it is likely that the defender will be standing in a similar position if attacked unexpectedly. The attacker then announces the target area, in this case *jodan* (upper attack). He then steps forward and performs a lunge punch to the face as the defender steps backward and blocks with a left rising block (Fig. 2). Note that in all these drills the defender moves to the weak side of his opponent, placing his body as far away from the strong side as possible. The attacker then steps in twice more and executes two additional attacks to the face. These are both blocked with rising blocks by the defender (Figs.

Figure 4

Figure 5

3–4). After blocking the third lunge punch, the defender counters with a punch to the midsection (Fig. 5). Both sides then resume the natural position, and the defender assumes the role of attacker.

Figure 6

Figure 7

Figure 8

Drill 2 (Figs. 6–10)

This drill is the same as the one above except that the target area is the solar plexus, and the block used is the outside forearm block.

Figure 9

Figure 10

Figure 11

Figure 12

Figure 13

Drill 3 (Figs. 11–15)

This drill is the same as the two above with the exception that the target area is the lower abdomen and the block is the downward block.

Figure 14

Figure 15

Figure 16

Figure 17

Figure 18

Drill 4 (Figs. 16–20)

In this drill the attacker executes three techniques: a lunge punch to the face, a lunge punch to the midsection, and finally a front kick to the lower body. The defender executes a rising block, a forearm block, and finally a downward block before counterpunching.

This is only a sampling of the drill possibilities, and all blocks and techniques may be used in the drills. For example, the attacker may use three consecutive front kicks in the attack. The defender may utilize any block that is suitable for each attack and may counter with punches, strikes, or kicks. Unlimited variations are possible in this drill, and it may be expanded to five or seven steps if space permits.

While variety in this drill is desirable, the underlying lesson must be kept in mind. This is a drill that trains

Figure 19

Figure 20

basic body movement, basic blocks and attacks, and perhaps most important of all teaches proper distancing. Instructors utilizing this drill should emphasize this to students continually so that they may adjust their distance to deliver the strongest possible counterattack.

Figure 21

Figure 22

Figure 23

One-Attack Sparring

One-attack sparring, sometimes called *kihon kumite* or *ippon kumite*, is a bit more advanced than three-attack sparring. This is not because the techniques are harder to execute, but because it is more important to learn proper body movement and basic blocking and distancing prior to working on the one-attack drill. Since each drill has different points to emphasize, it should be noted that, in addition to basic blocking and countering, the one-attack drill also has other goals. They include decreasing the time between the block and punch (reaction time), use of linear and circular movement, and development of the principle of *ikken hissatsu*, the ability to finish an opponent with one strong, focused technique. Depicted here are some of the basic methods of training in one-attack sparring.

Drill 1 (Figs. 21–23)

After the students bow to each other at the beginning of the drill, the attacker (left side) steps back with his left leg and blocks down with his right hand. The defender stands in the natural stance (Fig. 21), anticipating the attack, which is announced by his adversary. The attacker then steps forward and executes a left lunge punch to the face, which is blocked by the defender, using a rising block (Fig. 22). The defender then follows through with a counterpunch to the midsection (Fig. 23).

Drill 2 (Figs. 24–26)

In this case the attack is a lunge punch to the midsection, and the block used is an outside forearm block.

Figure 24

Figure 25

Figure 26

Drill 3 (Figs. 27–29)

The attack is a lunge punch, and the defender uses an inside forearm block, followed by a counterpunch.

Figure 27

Figure 28

Figure 29

Drill 4 (Figs. 30–32)

In this case the attack is a punch to the lower abdomen, and the defense is a downward block followed by a counterpunch.

Figure 30

Figure 31

Figure 32

Drill 5 (Figs. 33–35)

The attacker executes a right lunge punch to the face (Fig. 34). The defender blocks it with a left, outside forearm block. He then counters his attacker with a right roundhouse elbow strike to the ribs (Fig. 35).

Figure 33

Figure 34   **Figure 35**

Drill 6 (Figs. 36–38)

Here the defender uses a knife-hand block in the back stance against the lunge punch to the stomach. He follows his block by shifting into the front stance and executing a counter-punch.

As demonstrated here, the defensive side and the attacking side have both used linear movement. A variation of the practice would see the defensive side pivoting on one foot and twisting his body out of the way in a circular movement, as demonstrated in the following sections. Both methods of defense should be practiced, utilizing all types of attacks and defenses. Although only hand attacks have been shown here, it is also necessary to use kicking techniques as well.

Figure 36   Figure 37

Figure 38

Drill 7 (Figs. 39–41)

The attacker (right) uses a right lunge punch to the face (Fig. 40), and the defender blocks with a high, outside forearm block. He then counters with a right counterpunch to the ribs (Fig. 41).

Figure 39

Figure 40

Figure 41

Drill 8 (Figs. 42–44)

The attacker executes a right lunge punch to the face, and the defender steps back with his right foot and blocks using a right extended knife-hand block (Fig. 43). He then counters with a roundhouse kick to the solar plexus (Fig. 44).

Figure 42

Figure 43

Figure 44

Drill 9 (Figs. 45–47)

The attacker executes a right lunge punch to the midsection. The defender steps to the left with his left foot, assuming the back stance and blocking with the right knife-hand block (Fig. 46). He then counters with a right front snap-kick to the midsection (Fig. 47).

Figure 45

Figure 46

Figure 47

Figure 48

Figure 49

Figure 50

Drill 10 (Figs. 48–52)

The attacker executes a right lunge punch to the midsection, and the defender steps directly to the right and raises his left knee in preparation for a side thrust-kick (Fig. 49). He blocks using an extended knife-hand block. After executing a side thrust-kick to his opponent's midsection (Fig. 50), he withdraws his kicking leg, pivots on his left foot, and attacks his opponent with a right roundhouse kick to the head (Figs. 51–52).

Figure 51

Figure 52

Drill 11 (Figs. 53–55)

The attacker executes a right lunge punch to the midsection. The defender steps out to the left, assuming the sanchin stance and blocking with a right circular block (Fig. 54). He then counters with a left palm-heel strike to the jaw (Fig. 55).

Figure 53

Figure 54

Figure 55

Drill 12 (Figs. 56–58)

The attacker executes a right lunge punch to the midsection. The defender pivots on his left foot into the straddle stance and blocks with a high, outside forearm block, using his left arm (Fig. 57). He then counters with a left back-fist strike to the solar plexus (Fig. 58).

Figure 56

Figure 57

Figure 58

Drill 13 (Figs. 59–61)

The attacker executes a right lunge punch to the face, and the defender pivots on his left leg and assumes a straddle stance (Fig. 60). He blocks using a high, outside forearm block. He then counters with a left elbow thrust to the ribs (Fig. 61).

Figure 59

Figure 60

Figure 61

Drill 14 (Figs. 62–64)

The attacker executes a right lunge punch to the face, and the defender pivots on his left foot and performs a left, outside forearm block (Fig. 63). He then counters with a right ridge-hand strike to the neck (Fig. 64).

Figure 62

Figure 63

Figure 64

Figure 65

Figure 66

Figure 67

One-Step Two-Attack Sparring

In this type of sparring drill, the defender is faced with a combination of attacks that have to be dealt with consecutively prior to initiating a counterattack. For beginners it is generally best if the sequence of defensive moves consists of a first block, a second block, and then a counterattack. For more advanced practitioners, it is desirable to block the first attack and then simultaneously block and counter the second attack. This provides good training in timing and dealing with combinations.

Drill 1 (Figs. 65–68)

The attacker on the right steps forward and initiates an attack to the face with his right hand, followed by a counterpunch to the midsection with his left. The defensive side blocks the first attack with a left rising block (Fig. 66) and then brings his left arm downward and across, blocking the second punch with an outside forearm block (Fig. 67). He then follows with a counterpunch to the midsection of his opponent (Fig. 68).

Figure 68

Figure 69

Figure 70

Figure 71

Drill 2 (Figs. 69–73)

The attacker uses the same attack, that is, a lunge punch to the face followed by a counterpunch to the midsection. In this case the defender has blocked the face punch with a rising block (Fig. 70) and then used the same arm to sweep downward and outward, blocking his opponent's midsection attack with a downward block (Fig. 71). He then counters with a kick using his front leg (Fig. 72), followed by a right punch to the midsection (Fig. 73).

Numerous combinations of attacks may be practiced, using punches and kicks, and the defensive side may use any number of combinations in countering them.

Figure 72

Figure 73

Plate 17 A variety of techniques may be employed in semifree-sparring. Here, the side thrust-kick is used as a counterattack.

Semifree-Sparring

Semifree-sparring (*jiyu ippon kumite*) is a method of practicing fighting that is halfway between basic drilling and all-out free-fighting. Both players move around freely; however, one player is designated as the attacker and one as the defender. The method of attack is prearranged, although variations of prearrangement are possible. In the most common variation, the attacker simply indicates that he will execute a single lunge punch or other attack to a specific target. The defender then has only one attack to cope with. The attacker may use any attack with the hands or feet, and the defender is free to block and counter in any way possible. A variation on the theme has the attacker announcing the target area, but not the method of attack. Again, many methods of practice are possible. Presented here is the most basic, with the attacker indicating the method of attack and using first a lunge punch to the face, then a lunge punch to the midsection, a front kick, a side thrust-kick, and finally a roundhouse kick. The defender uses basic body shifting, blocking, and punching attacks in his defense. However, any means of blocking and counterattacking is acceptable, providing the counterblow is powerful enough to stop the opponent with that single technique.

Drill 1 (Figs. 74–76)

Both fighters face each other in free-sparring stances (Fig. 74). The attacker (right) steps forward and attacks with a right lunge punch to the face (Fig. 75). The defender shifts to his right and blocks with a left punching block to the face, and then follows with a right counterpunch to the midsection (Fig. 76).

Figure 74

Figure 75

Figure 76

Drill 2 (Figs. 77–79)

The fighters face each other in free-sparring stances (Fig. 77). The attacker (right) attacks with a right lunge punch to the midsection (Fig. 78). The defender shifts to his left in the front stance and blocks with a left outside forearm block. He then follows with a right counterpunch to the ribs of his attacker (Fig. 79).

Figure 77

Figure 78

Figure 79

Drill 3 (Figs. 80–82)

The fighters face each other in free-sparring stances (Fig. 80). The attacker (right) attacks with a right lunge punch to the face (Fig. 81). The defender shifts to the left and blocks with a high outside forearm block, and then counters with a right counterpunch to the ribs (Fig. 82).

Figure 80

Figure 81

Figure 82

Drill 4 (Figs. 83–85)

The fighters face each other in free-sparring stances (Fig. 83). The attacker (right) attacks with a front thrust-kick to the midsection (Fig. 84). The defender blocks with a sweeping forearm block. He then counters with a counterpunch to the ribs (Fig. 85).

Figure 83

Figure 84

Figure 85

Drill 5 (Figs. 86–88)

The fighters face each other in sparring stances (Fig. 86). The attacker (right) attacks with a side thrust-kick to the chest (Fig. 87). The defender shifts to the left and blocks with a left outside forearm block. He follows through with a counter-punch to the side (Fig. 88).

Figure 86

Figure 87

Figure 88

Drill 6 (Figs. 89–91)

The fighters face each other in sparring stances (Fig. 89). The attacker (right) attacks with a right roundhouse kick to the head (Fig. 90). The defender shifts to the right and blocks with a left inside forearm block. He then follows with a right counterpunch to the midsection (Fig. 91).

Figure 89

Figure 90

Figure 91

Figure 92

Figure 93

Figure 94

Direction-Reversing Drills

Since most fighters are capable of moving forward faster than their opponents can move backward, it follows that the fighter who initiates the attack and presses forward should have an advantage. In many cases, this is true, and it presents a problem for the fighter who allows his opponent to take the initiative. The solution to the problem is to stop the attack and drive the attacker back, taking the initiative away from him and putting him on the defensive. This is what is meant by direction reversing.

Figure 95

Although this is difficult to perform in actual combat, it is possible if the fighter trains thoroughly in rapid direction-reversing techniques. Required for success in this type of fighting is a strong, basic stance and the ability to shift backward and forward quickly.

Drill 1 (Figs. 92–96)

This is a basic method of practicing the direction-reversing pattern. In Figure 92 the fighter has assumed a

Figure 96

sparring stance with his right foot forward. He steps back (Fig. 93) and performs a rising block with his left hand, followed by a right counterpunch to the midsection (Fig. 94). He then kicks with his right leg, stepping forward as he kicks (Fig. 95) and, as his right foot comes down in the front stance, performs a left counterpunch (Fig. 96).

Drill 2 (Figs. 97–100)

This is similar to Drill 1 but without the use of the kick. It presupposes that the opponent is at closer range and may not be attacked with a kick. The fighter begins in the sparring stance (Fig. 97) and then steps back with his left foot, executing a right rising block (Fig. 98), followed by a left counterpunch (Fig. 99). He then steps forward with his left foot and executes a right counterpunch (Fig. 100).

Figure 97   Figure 98

Figure 99   Figure 100

Drill 3 (Figs. 101–104)

The fighter responds to a kicking attack by stepping back and performing a downward block (Fig. 102), followed by a counterpunch (Fig. 103). He then steps forward and executes another counterpunch (Fig. 104).

Figure 101

Figure 102

Figure 103

Figure 104

Drill 4 (Figs. 105–108)

The fighter stands in the right front stance (Fig. 105). He steps back with his right foot and stops his opponent's attack by using a jab to the face (Fig. 106). This is immediately followed by a right counterpunch to the midsection (Fig. 107). The direction of the fight is reversed as he steps forward with his right foot and executes a left counterpunch to the midsection (Fig. 108).

Although a number of basic moves have been used here, there is no reason why other techniques may not be utilized. What is necessary, however, is a strong stance and counter that will stop the attacker's forward advance and make it necessary for him to take a step backward.

Figure 105　　　　　　Figure 106

Figure 107　　　　　　Figure 108

Two-Man Direction-Reversing Drills

After training in the basic movements of direction reversing, it is necessary to practice them against an opponent. Depicted here are several drills that will aid in developing this type of movement.

Drill 1 (Figs. 109–115)

In this drill, the fighters face each other in a sparring stance, both with the left leg forward (Fig. 109). The fighter on the right steps forward and executes a right lunge punch to the face, and at the same time the fighter on the left steps back and executes a punch to the face with his right hand (Fig. 110).

Figure 109

Figure 110

Figure 111

Figure 112

Figure 113

Figure 114

Both fighters then follow up with counterpunches to the mid-section (Fig. 111). They then resume the sparring stance by bringing their hands to the position shown (Fig. 112). It is then the turn of the fighter on the left to initiate the attack, which he does by stepping forward with his left foot and performing a left lunge punch to the face (Fig. 113). At the same time he does this his opponent steps back with his right foot and executes a left jab to the face. Both fighters then counterpunch to each other's midsection at the same time (Fig. 114). They then resume the sparring stance by bringing their hands to the positions shown (Fig. 115).

The key to deriving the maximum benefit from this drill is to punch twice in rapid succession, just as in sparring. As soon as the fighter on the left has stepped back and executed his two punches (Figs. 110–111), he must return to the sparring position and immediately step forward to attack his opponent (Figs. 112–114). This is a very rapid drill, with the emphasis on changing direction quickly.

Figure 115

Figure 116

Figure 117

Figure 118

Drill 2 (Figs. 116–120)

Both fighters face each other in sparring stances, left legs forward (Fig. 116). The fighter on the right initiates the attack by stepping forward with his right leg and punching to the face with his right hand (Fig. 117). The fighter on the left has simply shifted backward and blocked with a left rising block. The defensive side then follows with a right counterpunch (Fig. 118) and then steps quickly forward with his right foot as his opponent retreats, simultaneously executing a left punch to the midsection (Fig. 119). Both fighters then return to the ready position (Fig. 120).

Figure 119

Figure 120

Drill 3 (Figs. 121–123)

The fighters face each other in the sparring stance, with their left legs forward (Fig. 120). The fighter on the right initiates the attack with a right front kick (Fig. 121), which is blocked as the fighter on the left shifts backward and blocks with a left downward block. He then counters with a right punch to the midsection (Fig. 122) and steps quickly forward, executing a left punch to the midsection (Fig. 123).

Figure 121

Figure 122

Figure 123

Drill 4 (Figs. 124–127)

The fighters face each other, the defender (left) in the natural stance and the attacker (right) in the left front stance (Fig.
124). The attacker steps forward with his right foot and executes a right lunge punch to the face as the defender steps
backward with his right foot and executes a left rising block
(Fig. 125). The defender (left) then steps forward and executes
a right lunge punch to the midsection and the attacker steps
back with his right foot and performs a left outside forearm
block (Fig. 126). The attacker (right) then executes a right
counterpunch to the midsection (Fig. 127).

Figure 124	Figure 125

Figure 126	Figure 127

Drill 5 (Figs. 128–131)

The two fighters face each other, the defender (left) in the natural stance and the attacker (right) in the left front stance (Fig. 128). The attacker steps forward and performs a right lunge punch to the midsection (Fig. 129) as the defender steps back with his right foot and performs a left outside forearm block. The defender (left) then steps forward with his right foot and executes a right lunge punch to the face as the attacker (right) steps backward with his right foot and performs a left rising block (Fig. 130). The attacker (right) then counters with a right counterpunch to the midsection (Fig. 131).

Figure 128

Figure 129

Figure 130

Figure 131

Body-Shifting Drills

The ability to shift one's body quickly and effectively in the course of combat can often mean the difference between victory and defeat. Such movements, involving hip shifting, make it possible to change direction, alternate techniques, and initiate strong countermoves. Demonstrated here are several drills designed to aid in developing hip-shifting ability.

Drill 1 (Figs. 132–134)

The defender stands in the natural position, awaiting his attacker's first move (Fig. 132). As the attacker steps forward with a lunge punch to the face, the defender shifts backward with his right foot (Fig. 133), blocking his opponent's attack with an extended, right knife-hand block. He then follows with a right roundhouse kick to the head (Fig. 134).

Figure 132

Figure 133

Figure 134

Drill 2 (Figs. 135–137)

In this defensive maneuver, the hip is used to shift the body at a 45-degree angle to the left as the attacker steps forward with a lunge punch (Fig. 136). The defender uses a downward block and then follows with a roundhouse kick to the midsection, using the front leg (Fig. 137).

Figure 135

Figure 136

Figure 137

Drill 3 (Figs. 138–141)

A more complex type of hip shift is demonstrated here. As the attacker steps forward with a front kick, the defender evades the attack by shifting his left foot back almost to the right (Figs. 139–140), reversing his hip position, and counterkicking with his right leg (Fig. 141).

Figure 138

Figure 139

Figure 140

Figure 141

Drill 4 (Figs. 142–144)

This hip-shifting movement is similar to that of Drill 3; however, in this case the defender evades a side thrust-kick (Fig. 143) and counters with a roundhouse kick (Fig. 144).

Figure 142

Figure 143

Figure 144

Drill 5 (Figs. 145–147)

In response to the punching attack with his opponent's right hand, the defender shifts his left foot backward to adjust distance (Fig. 146), simultaneously executing an extended, left knife-hand block, and then steps forward with a lunge punch to his opponent's midsection (Fig. 147).

Figure 145

Figure 146

Figure 147

Figure 148

Figure 149

Figure 150

Figure 151

Figure 152

Multiple-Attacker Drills

In addition to training against one attacker, it is necessary to practice defending against several opponents. This is because karate was developed as a defensive art and not a sport. One never knows when one will be attacked by several assailants at a time. Training with an attacker in front and in back or on both sides will assist in developing the self-defense skills of the karate practitioner. Although these drills demonstrate defenses against punching attacks, defense against kicking attacks should also be practiced.

Drill 1 (Figs. 148–152)

In this drill the defender is faced with attackers in front and in back of him (Fig. 148). He blocks the first attacker's punch with a left, outside, forearm block and then counters to the midsection with a right counterpunch (Figs. 149–150). Turning to face the attacker from the rear, he executes a right inside forearm block to stop the punching attack and then finishes his opponent with a counterpunch to the midsection (Figs. 151–152). It is essential to practice turning movements during basic training in order to maintain balance and a strong stance in this drill.

Drill 2 (Figs. 153–157)

The attacker in front executes a right lunge punch to the face
(Fig. 154), which is blocked with a left rising block and countered with a right, rising elbow strike to the chin (Fig. 155).
The defender then twists and blocks the punching attack from
the rear using an extended, right knife-hand block (Fig. 156).
This is followed by a right back thrust-kick to his opponent's
midsection (Fig. 157).

Figure 153

Figure 154

Figure 155

Figure 156

Figure 157

Drill 3 (Figs.158–163)

As the attacker in front punches to his face, the defender steps back with his right foot and executes an extended knife-hand block with his right hand (Fig. 159). He then counters with a roundhouse kick to the head, using his right leg (Fig.160). Continuing his movement, the defender steps forward and to the right side of the first attacker, then turns to meet the second attacker, who is dispatched with a right front kick (Figs.161–163).

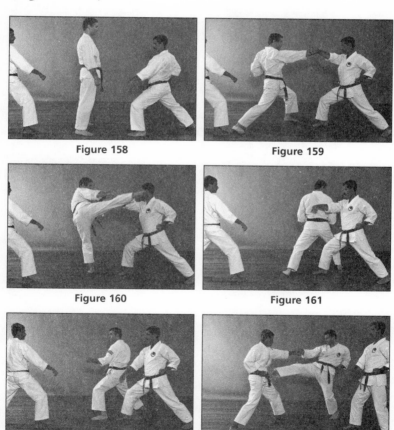

Figure 158

Figure 159

Figure 160

Figure 161

Figure 162

Figure 163

Drill 4 (Figs.164–167)

Anticipating the first attack, the defender simultaneously steps forward and punches to his opponent's face as he deflects the attacker's punch with his left hand (Fig. 165). He then turns and blocks his second attacker's punch with a sweeping, left knife-hand block (Fig. 166) and continues to turn, finishing his opponent with a right counterpunch (Fig.167).

Figure 164   Figure 165

Figure 166   Figure 167

Drill 5 (Figs. 168–173)

The defender (center) has opponents on both sides (Fig. 168). The opponent to his left attacks with a right lunge punch to the face, and the defender drops into a straddle stance and blocks with a high, outside forearm block, using his left arm (Fig. 169). He then follows his block with a left, side elbow thrust to his attacker's ribs (Fig. 170). A second assailant attacks with a right lunge punch to the face. The defender blocks with a right, extended knife-hand block (Fig. 171). He then grasps his attacker's right wrist with his left hand and pulls him forward as he executes a right side thrust-kick to the midsection (Figs. 172–173).

Figure 168

Figure 169

Figure 170

Figure 171

Figure 172

Figure 173

Drill 6 (Figs. 174–178)

The defender has attackers on both sides (Fig. 174). The attacker to his left attacks with a right lunge punch to the face. The defender twists his body clockwise and blocks with a right, extended knife-hand block (Fig. 175). He then counters with a right roundhouse kick to the head (Fig. 176). Without

Figure 174

placing his foot on the ground, he executes a right back thrust-kick to the chest of the second assailant who begins to move towards him (Figs. 177–178).

Figure 175

Figure 176

Figure 177

Figure 178

Drill 7 (Figs. 179–182)

The defender has attackers on both sides (Fig. 179). The attacker to his left executes a right lunge punch to the face, and the defender steps forward with his left foot into a front stance, blocks with a left sweeping block, and simultaneously counters with a right ridge-hand to the neck (Fig. 180). The attacker on his right executes a right lunge punch to the head and the defender blocks with a right, extended knife-hand block while standing in the straddle stance (Fig. 181). He immediately counters with a right knife-hand strike to the ribs (Fig. 182).

Figure 179

Figure 180

Figure 181

Figure 182

Drill 8 (Figs. 183–187)

The defender has attackers on both sides (Fig. 183). The attacker on his left executes a right lunge punch to the face, and the defender shifts into a straddle stance and simultaneously blocks with a left, sweeping block and counters with a right punch to the ribs (Fig. 184). The second attacker approaches from the right and executes a right lunge punch to the face. As he does this, the defender shifts his body into the left front stance and blocks with a right, extended knife-hand block (Figs. 185–186). He then grasps his opponent's wrist and pulls him forward as he performs a front thrust-kick to the stomach (Fig. 187).

Figure 183

Figure 184

Figure 185

Figure 186

Figure 187

CHAPTER SIX
Kata

Kata Development

Kata, in the present day, is practiced according to a predetermined method. That is to say that one kata practiced by different individuals is supposed to be exactly the same, facilitating judgment during kata competition and rank competitions. This supposition is an error. A cursory examination of the kata indicates that throughout many systems of karate, kata that have common origins are practiced differently. Thus in ten different karate systems, the *kata Bassai Dai* will be practiced in ten different ways. Which is the right way? Why are there so many different ways?

Common sense would indicate that the masters never intended kata to be practiced in exactly the same way in all conditions. If an instructor had five students of varying body type and ability, then those five individuals would perform the kata differently. A student with a stiff hip might have to perform the side kick to the knee while another individual with greater hip flexibility might aim the kick higher. Kata also developed differently according to school and region. There is no reason for kata to be consistent in performance except for matters of judging in tournament and exams. Therefore the current system of kata practice is wrong — it was never intended to be taught as it is in the present day. Under these conditions kata loses its adaptability to the individual, and therefore he derives no benefit from it. It is far better to allow individual differences in performance of the kata. This may seem to be quite contrary to tradition; however, it is more in keeping with tradition than the current practice. Following that premise, why shouldn't individual karate practitioners simply devise their own kata and disregard the old forms of training? This too would be an error. The original intent of the movements in the forms must be studied. Many of them were proven in actual combat, although no records of this exist. What is suggested here is that there must be greater variation in the manner in which individuals perform a given kata. That is possible and beneficial; however, only after the individual has studied a form long enough to appreciate the meaning of the movements should he be allowed to attempt variations. Beginners attempting to do this would simply miss the point entirely and lose what little exposure they had to true karate.

Understanding Kata

It is not unusual for beginning students of karate to ask about practical applications of karate technique for specific self-defense situations. These are reasonable questions; however, they demonstrate a complete lack of knowledge about the principles of fighting. Karate masters of the past centuries devised a number of katas that have been passed on to the present day. In general, these katas may be divided into two general classifications: those belonging to either the *Shorin* or the *Shorei* tradition.

Shorin katas were developed by karate masters who believed that karate fighters should move quickly and that the ability to shift, dodge, and counter rapidly was of the utmost importance. As a result, the katas of the Shorin tradition exhibit a great deal of rapid movement. Among the katas belonging to this tradition are *Empi, Kanku, Bassai, Nijushiho,* and *Gojushiho.*

Shorei katas contain an emphasis on power in technique and were developed by karate masters who probably thought that strength was superior to rapid movement. Accordingly, they practiced methods of developing power through breathing and other exercises. Katas belonging to this group are *Hangetsu, Jutte, Jion,* and *Sochin.*

Most schools of karate that have been developed in the present century hold that the exclusion of either type of technique is an error, and therefore they practice a combination of both. Master Gichin Funakoshi, the founder of *Shotokan* karate, recommended the practice of fifteen basic forms, choosing what he considered to be the essential ones from each tradition. They are: *Heian Shodan, Heian Nidan, Heian Sandan, Heian Yodan, Heian Godan, Tekki Shodan, Tekki Nidan, Tekki Sandan, Bassai Dai, Kanku Dai, Empi, Gankaku, Jutte, Hangetsu,* and *Jion.*

These forms have been modified and individualized over the years; however, their basic movements are still designed for self-defense situations. To the uninitiated, some of the basic movements are incomprehensible, while others have an obvious application to a specific attack. To understand the meaning of each movement in a kata is to reach the first level of proficiency in that form, assuming that the practitioner is capable of executing each movement in the kata correctly. This presupposes a great deal of practice of the individual form.

In the past, the method of learning kata differed from that of the present day. Today, students learn the basic forms in a relatively short time, sometimes spending only a few months on one kata before learning another. Compared to the past method of training in kata, this is quite superficial and leads to a minimal amount of understanding of the kata and of self-defense moves in general. Prior to the present day it was necessary to

Figure 1

Figure 2

Figure 3

Figure 4

Figure 5

Figure 6

spend several years specializing in each form in order to gain the most knowledge from it. Repetitive training focused on a single kata is still the method of practice in some of the more traditional karate organizations; however, in many of the more modern, sports-oriented karate *dojos*, it is not. This has led to a lack of good training in self-defense movements. As an example, consider one of the simplest movements found in kata, the downward block in the front stance.

Downward blocking techniques are found in many popular katas, among them Heian Shodan, Heian Nidan, Empi, and Jion. The first two forms mentioned are basic, while the last two are considered to be on the intermediate level. Figures 1 through 3 show the beginning movement of the kata Heian Shodan, although the same movement is found in many other katas. The performer steps to the left and performs a left downward block in the front stance. To a beginning student, this is an obvious attempt to block a punch, as demonstrated in Figures 4 and 5. However, while such an explanation is true, the move also has a number of other applications.

To apply this movement to a self-defense situation, imagine an opponent approaching from the left side (Figs. 6–7) and grasping the jacket. The defender grab his attacker's wrist, steps into a front stance, and executes the

Figure 7

Figure 8   **Figure 9**

Figure 10   **Figure 11**

Figure 12

downward blocking movement, striking his attacker in the elbow and breaking his arm (Figs. 8–9). The movement is performed in the same manner as the block against a punch, but in this instance it is used to break free from a hold.

In Figures 10 and 11 an opponent approaches from the left and attempts a choke. The defender steps toward his opponent and this time uses the motion as an attack, striking his opponent's groin with a bottom-fist strike (Fig. 12).

One of the more common explanations for the movement is to view it as a downward block against a kick, as shown in Figures 13 and 14. This explanation and the first one cited are probably the most common interpretations that beginners usually learn.

Figure 13

Figure 14

It is also possible to use the same movement as a throwing technique. In this case, the left leg is placed behind the attacker, and the downward movement of the arm used to throw him to the ground (Figs. 15–19).

Figure 15

Figure 16

Figure 17

Figure 18

The bottom-fist may also be used to strike the opponent's temple as he attempts to grasp the legs, as a wrestler might do. As shown here, the technique is a bit higher than normally performed in the kata, since the target area is higher (Figs. 20–22).

Figure 19

Figure 20

Figure 21

Figure 22

Figure 23

Figure 24

Figure 25

Figure 26

In a final series of photos the attacker again tries to choke the defender, who steps forward and grasps his opponent's testicles, following with the downward blocking movement. This combination of pulling with the right hand and sweeping downward with the left is used to throw the attacker to the ground (Figs. 23–26).

When karate instructors speak of the "hidden meaning" of the kata, it is this to which they refer. If one assiduously practices a particular kata for an extended length of time, the tactics possible from a given movement are expanded. The more feeling that a practitioner has for a particular move, the more knowledge will be gained from it.

Thus we have an answer for those who demand self-defense movements for specific attacks. Since it is impossible to know just how such an attack may be attempted, it will be impossible to train thousands of possible responses. If the basic movement and basic principle are understood, then that movement may be adapted to meet any situation. This is why such diligent practice of kata is so important and one of the reasons that karate masters in the past trained intensively in kata and basics. It must be remembered that sport karate is a relatively new development, and masters of old were more likely to be in a position of having to defend themselves with karate techniques. In order to accomplish their goal, they devised and practiced kata. The years spent in practice of those forms were considered invaluable for self-defense ability. They still are.

Kanku-Dai

Kanku Dai is the modern Japanese name for an older Okinawan kata. Its original name, *Kushanku*, was derived from that of a Chinese martial artist who came to Okinawa in the eighteenth century. An example of the Shorin school of flexible, rapid movement, it is characterized by dodging attacks using crouching methods as well as a jumping kick. To perform Kanku Dai:

Begin in the informal attention stance and perform the opening bow (Figs. 27–29). Assume the ready position (Fig. 30). Place the open hands in front of the body with the fingertips and thumb tips touching, so that an opening is formed between the hands (Fig. 31). Slowly raise the hands in front

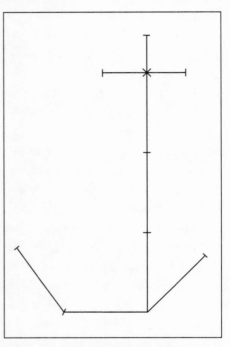

Plate 15   Embusen — Kanku Dai

of the body, as shown, and look through the opening between the hands (Fig. 32). Continue the movement by bringing the hands outward and to the sides, forming a circle (Figs. 33–34). The hands are brought together in front of the body with the edge of the left open hand pressed against the palm of the right open hand, near the junction of the fourth and fifth fingers.

Look to the left, step 90 degrees to the left with the left foot, assuming the left back stance, and bring the left hand upward and outward, performing a left back-hand block (Fig. 35). Turn clockwise 180 degrees to the rear and perform another back-hand block, this time with the right hand (Fig. 36). The stance is the back stance. These first two moves are done quickly, almost as though they were one. Slowly face front and bring the left foot up to the right, as shown. Cross the hands in preparation for an extended knife-hand block with the left hand (Fig. 37). Slowly extend the left arm and perform a left, vertical, knife-hand block (Fig. 38). Punch to the midsection with the right hand (Fig. 39). Shift the left foot to the side and perform a right inside forearm block in the front stance (Fig. 40). Snap the hips in a clockwise motion, assuming a natural stance, and execute a left punch to the midsection (Fig. 41). Step to the right with the right foot, executing a left, inside, forearm block with the left arm in the front stance (Fig. 42). Bring the left foot to the center-line of the body, raise the right foot to the left knee in preparation for a right side snap-kick, and place the left fist on top of the right (Fig. 43). You have turned 90 degrees in a clockwise movement to the right. Execute a right side snap-kick and a right back-fist strike (Fig. 44). Withdraw the kicking foot to the knee then step back down with the right foot, assuming a right back stance and executing a left knife-hand block (Figs. 45–46). You have turned 180 degrees in a clockwise movement from the direction of the kick. Step forward with the right foot and execute a right knife-hand block in the right back stance (Fig. 47). Step forward and execute a left knife-hand block in the left back stance (Fig. 48). Step forward in the right front stance and kiai as you execute a right spear-hand thrust to the midsection (Fig. 49). As you perform the thrusting movement with the right hand, place the back of the left open hand under the right elbow, as if performing a pressing block with the open hand.

Turn to the rear 180 degrees in a counterclockwise movement, simultaneously executing a left sweeping block to the outside of the lower body and right knife-hand strike to the neck (Figs. 50–51). The left hand continues around and is used as an upward block on the left side of the head. (Figure 51A shows this move from the side.) Execute a right front snap-kick (Fig. 52). (Figure 52A is the side view.) Pivoting on the left foot 180 degrees in a counterclockwise movement, place the right foot on the ground in a back stance and simultaneously perform a left downward block and a right, high, inside forearm block (Fig. 53). (Figure 53A shows the side view.) Twist into the front stance, performing a right knife-hand strike to the groin and a left knife-hand block by the side of the neck Fig. 54). (Figure 54A is the side view.) Slowly withdraw the left foot and perform a left downward block (Fig. 55) The stance is then the left L stance. Slide the left foot forward into the left front stance, simultaneously performing a right knife-hand strike to the neck and a left, open-handed block, as shown (Fig. 56). Shift the weight to the left foot and perform a right front snap-kick (Fig. 57). Pivot on the left foot 180 degrees counterclockwise to the left, withdrawing the kicking foot (Fig. 58). Step down and back with the kicking foot, assuming a left back stance and performing simultaneous left downward and high, right, inside forearm blocks (Fig. 59). Twist forward into the left front stance and perform a right knife-hand strike to the groin and a left knife-hand block by the right side of the neck (Fig. 60). Slowly withdraw the left foot into the left L stance and perform a left downward block (Fig. 61). Shift the weight to the right foot and perform a left side snap-kick and back-fist strike (Fig. 62). Step down into the left front stance and strike the left palm with a right, roundhouse elbow strike (Fig. 63). You have turned 90 degrees to the left in a counterclockwise movement. Withdraw the right foot to the left knee and place the right fist on top of the left side of the body (Fig. 64). Execute a right side snap-kick and a right back-fist strike (Fig. 65); as your right foot comes down in a front stance, strike your right palm with a left roundhouse elbow strike (Fig. 66). Turn 180 degrees counterclockwise into the back stance and perform a left knife-hand block in the left back stance (Fig. 67). Step 45 degrees forward and to the right as you execute a right knife-hand block in the back stance (Fig. 68). Pivot 135 degrees clockwise on the left foot, assuming the back stance and blocking with the right knife-hand block (Fig. 69). Step 45 degrees forward and to the left as you execute a left knife-hand block in the back stance (Fig. 70).

Slide the left foot over 45 degrees to the left in a counterclockwise movement, assuming the front stance. As you shift your feet, simultaneously perform a left rising block with the open hand and a right knife-hand strike to the neck (Fig. 71). Perform a right front snap-kick (Fig. 72), then take a sliding step forward with the right foot (Fig. 73). Bring the left foot behind the right as you perform a right back-fist strike to the face (Fig. 74). (Figure 74A is the side view.)

Keeping the right foot in place, step back with the left foot into a front stance, performing a right, inside, forearm block as you move your left foot (Fig. 75). (Figure 75A is the side view.) In place, punch first with the left and then with the right fist to the midsection (Figs. 76–77). (Figures 76A and 77A are side views.) Turn 180 degrees to the rear in a counterclockwise movement by pivoting on the left leg. As you do this, strike the left palm with the right forearm as you punch with the right fist (Fig. 78). (Figure 78A is a side view.) Let the body fall forward, placing both hands and the right foot on the floor (Fig. 79). (Figure 79A is the side view.) Turn 180 degrees to the rear in a back stance (counterclockwise), performing a left, augmented downward block with the left knife-hand (Fig. 80). (Figure 80A is the side view.) Step forward in the back stance and perform a right knife-hand block (Fig. 81). Pivot counterclockwise 225 degrees on the right foot, assuming the front stance and executing a left, inside forearm block (Fig. 82). In place, counterpunch to the midsection with the right hand (Fig. 83). Turn 180 degrees to the rear in a clockwise move and perform a right, inside forearm block in the front stance (Fig. 84). Alternately punch to the midsection with the left and right hands (Figs. 85–86).

Draw the right foot back to the left knee, pivoting 90 degrees to the right, and place the right fist on top of the left-hand side of the body (Fig. 87). Execute a right side snap-kick and a right back-fist strike (Fig. 88). Pivot 180 degrees clockwise on the left foot, step back into the left back stance, and perform a left knife-hand block (Figs. 89–90). Step forward and execute a right spear-hand thrust to the midsection (Fig. 91). The left hand is held under the right elbow, palm down. Pivot 225 degrees in a counterclockwise move, breaking the opponent's grasp on your right wrist and assuming the straddle stance as you execute a left back-fist strike to the face (Figs. 92–94). Shift both feet six inches to the left as you perform a left bottom-fist strike to the midsection (Figs. 95–96). Hit the left palm with a right, roundhouse, elbow strike (Fig. 97). Look to the right, bring the right fist on top of the left, and then execute a right downward block to the right side of the body (Figs. 98–99). (Figure 99A shows this from the side.) Pivot 180 degrees in a clockwise movement on the right foot, bringing the hands into the position shown. As you step down, perform a left downward block with the palm up and a high, right, inside forearm block with the palm toward the body (Figs. 100–101). (Figure 101A shows this from the front.) In place, perform a downward cross-block, with the right hand on the bottom (Fig. 102). Shift both feet inward to about shoulder width and perform an upward cross-block with the hands open (Fig. 103). Pivot 225 degrees in a clockwise movement on the right foot (Figs. 104–105). As you assume the new direction, step back with the left foot and bring both hands slowly to chest level (Fig. 106). When you do this movement, keep the hands crossed in a block, forming them into fists as they are brought downward.

Take off on the right foot, alternately performing a left and then a right jumping kick (Figs. 107–109). (Figures 107A and 109A show this from the side.) As you land in the right front stance, kiai as you perform a right back-fist strike to the face (Fig. 110). Pivot 180 degrees clockwise on the right foot, performing a scooping block with the right hand (Fig. 111). Bring both fists in a circular movement over the head and downward to the ready position (Figs. 112–114). Place the heels together and perform the ending bow (Figs. 115–117).

Figure 27   Figure 28   Figure 29

Figure 30   Figure 31   Figure 32

Figure 33   Figure 34   Figure 35

Figure 36   Figure 37   Figure 38

Figure 39   Figure 40   Figure 41

Figure 42   Figure 43   Figure 44

Figure 45   Figure 46   Figure 47

Figure 48   Figure 49   Figure 50

Figure 51   Figure 51A   Figure 52

Figure 52A   Figure 53   Figure 53A

Figure 54   Figure 54A   Figure 55

Figure 56   Figure 57   Figure 58

Figure 59

Figure 60

Figure 61

Figure 62

Figure 63

Figure 64

Figure 65

Figure 66

Figure 67

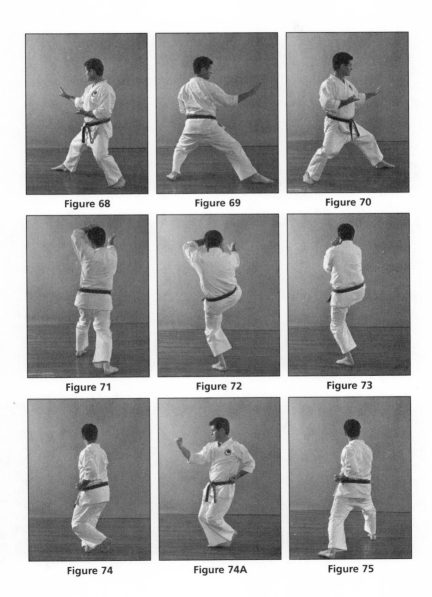

Figure 68   Figure 69   Figure 70

Figure 71   Figure 72   Figure 73

Figure 74   Figure 74A   Figure 75

Figure 75A   Figure 76   Figure 76A

Figure 77   Figure 77A   Figure 78

Figure 78A   Figure 79   Figure 79A

Figure 80   Figure 80A   Figure 81

Figure 82   Figure 83   Figure 84

Figure 85   Figure 86   Figure 87

Figure 88   Figure 89   Figure 90

Figure 91   Figure 92   Figure 93

Figure 94   Figure 95   Figure 96

Figure 97   Figure 98

Figure 99   Figure 99A   Figure 100

Figure 101   Figure 101A   Figure 102

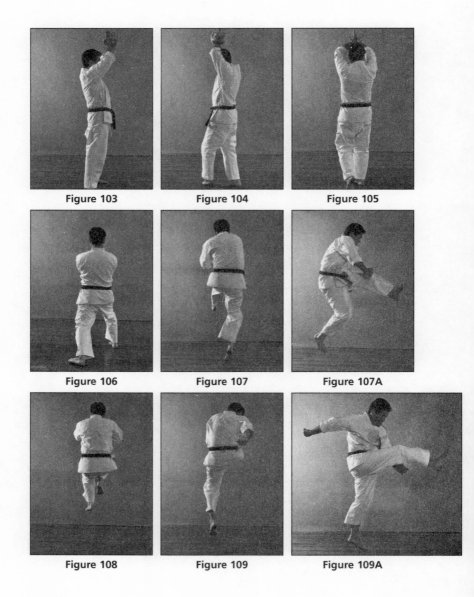

Figure 103   Figure 104   Figure 105

Figure 106   Figure 107   Figure 107A

Figure 108   Figure 109   Figure 109A

Figure 110 Figure 111 Figure 112

Figure 113 Figure 114 Figure 115

Figure 116 Figure 117

Figure 118

Figure 119

Figure 120

Figure 121

Figure 122

Figure 123

Kanku-Dai: Explanation of Moves

Move 35

An attacker advances from the left and executes a right lunge punch to the defender's head. The defender slides his left foot towards the attacker, assuming a back stance and simultaneously executing a left back-hand block (Figs. 118–119). He then counters his attacker with a left front kick to the stomach (Fig. 120).

Moves 37–42

An attacker approaches from the front and executes a left counterpunch to the midsection. The defender blocks using a left, extended knife-hand block (Fig. 121). The defender then counters with a right punch to the midsection (Fig. 122). The attacker punches with a right hand to the defender's midsection, and the defender blocks with a right, inside forearm block (Fig. 123). He then counters with a left punch to his attacker's ribs (Fig. 124). The attacker punches again, this time with his left hand, and the defender blocks with a left, inside forearm block (Fig. 125).

Figure 124

Figure 125

Figure 126

Figure 127

Figure 128

Figure 129

Figure 130

Figure 131

Moves 43–44

The attacker approaches from the defender's right side. He attacks with a right lunge punch to the face, and the defender blocks with a left back-fist strike and simultaneously kicks his ribs with a right side snap-kick (Fig. 126).

Moves 48–49

Faced with an advancing attacker to the front, the defender (right) steps forward and blocks with a pressing downward block (Figs. 127–128) and then attacks with a spear-hand thrust to the solar plexus (Fig. 129).

Moves 50–52

The defender (left) turns to his rear to meet an attacker who is executing a left counterpunch to the midsection. Deflecting the punch with a left, downward sweeping block, he counters with a right knife-hand strike to the neck (Figs. 130–131) and then follows with a right front kick to the face (Fig. 132).

Figure 132

Figure 133

Figure 134

Figure 135

Figure 136

Figure 137

Figure 138

Move 53

After kicking his opponent, the defender turns to his rear in the left back stance, facing a new attacker. The new attacker executes a right lunge punch, which the defender blocks, while simultaneously blocking a left face punch from the rear using a right inside forearm block (Fig. 133).

Move 54

The attacker in the front moves forward and executes a right lunge punch to the face. The defender deflects the punch with the palm of his right hand and simultaneously counters with a right knife-hand strike to the groin (Fig. 134).

Move 74

After kicking at his opponent, the defender (left) steps forward and executes a right back-fist strike to the face, sliding his right foot behind his left (Fig. 135).

Move 78

The defender, turning to meet an attack from the rear, simultaneously grabs his opponent's right wrist with his left hand and strikes him behind the elbow with his right forearm, breaking the arm (Fig. 136).

Moves 79–80

The defender dodges a kicking attack from the rear by dropping down on the floor, supporting himself on the palms of his hands (Fig. 137). He immediately rises and turns to meet the punching attack, using an augmented downward block with the knife-hand to defend himself (Fig. 138).

Figure 139

Figure 140

Figure 141

Figure 142

Figure 143

Figure 144

Moves 91–96

An opponent grasps the right wrist of the defender (Fig. 139). The defender turns counterclockwise into a straddle stance, breaking the hold and counter-attacking with a left back-fist strike to the head (Figs. 140–141). He then follows with a bottom-fist strike to the kidneys (Fig. 142).

Moves 100–105

The attacker executes a left lunge punch to the head. The defender shifts into the straddle stance and simultaneously blocks with a right forearm block and strikes his opponent's groin with his left fist (Fig. 143). As his opponent attempts a kick, he blocks using a downward cross-block (Fig. 144). His attacker then punches to the face with a left punch, and he stands up and blocks with an upward cross-block, using his open hands (Fig. 145). He then grasps his attacker's wrist and turns in a clockwise movement, simultaneously pulling the wrist down and breaking the elbow joint (Figs. 146–147).

Figure 145

Figure 146

Figure 147

Moves 110–113

An attackers approaches from the rear (Fig. 148) and attacks with a front kick. The defender turns and blocks, using a right scooping block (Fig. 149).

Figure 148   **Figure 149**